I Am An Overcomer, I Survived!

**A Collaboration Presented by:
Dr. Elaine Harvey**

© 2023 Dr. Elaine Harvey

Book Cover Design: Dr. Shadaria Allison | Nichol LeAnn Perricci, DNP Designs
Interior Book Design & Formatting: TamikaINK.com
Editor: TamikaINK.com

ALL RIGHTS RESERVED. No part of this book may be reproduced in any written, electronic, recording, or photocopying without written permission of the publisher or author. The exception would be in the case of brief quotations embodied in critical articles or reviews and pages where permission is specifically granted by the publisher or author.

LEGAL DISCLAIMER. Although the author has made every effort to ensure that the information in this book was correct at press time, the author does not assume hereby disclaim any liability to any party for loss, damage, or disruption caused by errors or missions, whether such errors or omissions result from negligence, accident, or any other cause.

Published By: Igniting The Flame Publishing

Library of Congress Cataloging-in-Publication Data has been applied for

ISBN: 9798377414773
PRINTED IN THE UNITED STATES OF AMERICA

Endorsement
By Dr. Michael Hunter

Dr. Pastor Elaine Harvey's anthology is "I Am An Overcomer, I Survived!" She's a woman of integrity and great faith; she is an encourager and a motivator with the gift to empower and uplift. As you read this book, you will be encouraged, your spirit shall be uplifted, and your life will be impacted in a miraculous way. Dr. Harvey is a woman of faith, an obedient servant of God, an excellent great mother, grandmother, a spiritual mentor to many, loving spirit, excellent leader.

Dr. Michael Hunter

Eagle's Rest Church,
The Living Word Telecast On Thursday night on The Word Network.

Endorsement
By Dr. Glen Allen Sr.

Sometimes, people live their lives in regret; however, that is not our story as the people of God. We understand that as disciples, we are given the power to overcome by the blood of the Lamb and by the word of our testimony. I Am An Overcomer "I Survived!" is a dynamic anthology that shows readers all over the world how to win and even overcome. This body of work is anointed, and all who would believe in Him through His word - they will overcome. As we minister the gospel to the world, we become witnesses to the truth and power of God (Jesus) and his Word!

Dr. Elaine Harvey is the Visionary of this impactful, great work: *I Am An Overcomer "I Survived."* She's a leader that is faithful, courageous, called, and runs with the vision God has given into her hands. I'm honored to endorse her and this book so that it reaches the masses around the world. Congratulations to you and every Author who wrote with you. Dr. Pastor Harvey, I want to say kudos and "job well done" on your inspiring project!

Apostle Dr. Glen Allen Sr.

Moto: Bringing truth back to our community one soul at a time.

Apostle Dr. Glen Allen Sr. is a man of honor, valor & Godly wisdom. He's spent over the last 40 years of his life serving God & God's people.

Refusing to allow anything to stop him on all fronts, Glen has trailblazed a credible path for those he serves in this great Gospel. Matching servant leadership with an incredible respect for the call upon his life he has preached Jesus and him crucified.

He has served as Senior Pastor of Lighthouse Apostolic Ministries of God Church for the last 23 years; and is the President of the nonprofit organization, L.A.M. Ministries, Inc. since January 2001.

He holds Ministerial Diploma in Biblical Studies from Destiny School of Ministry. Dr. Glen Allen Sr. graduated on 10/29/22 with the degree of: Doctor of Philosophy Christian Leadership and Business. Dr. Allen is also a 2X and International Bestselling Author from Workbook "Coach Drs" released December 2022 with global success.

Presiding Apostle of Lighthouse Apostolic Alliance establish 8/2022

Co-Owner: Igniting The Flame Publishing 3/2022

Co-Owner: Visionary Coaching & Consultant Group LLC 2/2019

Ordained as Bishop in International Alliance of Apostolic Ministries, Organization July 2019

Ordained as Bishop in June 2017 Pentecostal Power Organization

Ordained as Elder & Pastor in 9/1999 in Pentecostal Assembly of the World Organization

CEO/Owner of Little Lights Childcare & Learning Center 4/2004 - 9/2014

Dr. Glen Allen Sr. - Apostle. Bishop. Leader. Visionary. Organizer

Contact Information: Apostle Dr. Glen Allen Sr.

Lighthouse Apostolic Ministries of God Church

Email: lamministriesinc@aol.com

www.lamministriesinc.com

www.ignitingtheflamepublishing

Dedication

This book is dedicated to my son Enoch. I want you to know that with the Lord on our side, nothing is impossible if you believe. Don't give up on your dreams and goals. Keep the dream alive. Thank you for always believing in me and being the young man you are.

I love you so much! I pray the favor of God will continue to follow you all the days of your life.
Always keep your faith in the Lord!

Dr. Elaine Harvey

Acknowledgments

I want to give thanks to my Lord Jesus Christ. I would also like to give a special thanks to all of the Authors in this book for sharing your chapter and story to encourage and inspire people worldwide. Special thanks to my Publisher, Apostle Dr. Deborah Allen for all your hard work, commitment, and effort that you have spent helping this project succeed. The editing team and all those who are working behind the scheme. I thank the Lord for everyone, and I appreciate all your hard work and commitment to such a great accomplishment!

I want to thank everyone in Igniting the flame publishing company that played a significant part in completing this project. We are truly grateful to all of you for doing a great job!

Dr. Elaine Harvey

Table of Contents

Introduction By Dr. Elaine Harvey 13

Be Fierce, For You Are Destined To Overcome. By Dr. Deborah Allen 27

You Can Overcome Too By Ivy Caldwell 39

Woman Behind The Mask By Dr. Elizabeth Perkins.............. 51

Overcoming Difficult Situations By Taletha Morrison 61

A Great Work: Finishing Strong with No More Spiritual Miscarriage By Ricky James Allen-Callahan 67

Cancer Did Not Win...By LaKeisha J. Richards...................... 81

Surviving Divorce: Broken Vows Behind The Veil By Cheryl Richard... 91

Life's Afflictions By Cassandra Lang..................................... 103

Go On, Girl. You Are A Queen! By Felicia Mckoy-Laguerre 113

Live and Not Die By Dr. Juliet Pinder-McBride 125

Introduction
By Dr. Elaine Harvey

We all have gone through some storms and challenges throughout this journey. The authors of this collaboration, sharing their chapters on how they survived, are here to encourage and inspire everyone that with the Lord on our side, what was meant to take us out of here made us even stronger. We know that (Philippians 4:13) I can do all things through Christ who strengthened me. We all have we survived some challenging, painful situations, and we know it was God's hand.

That was in our lives, even through the good and bad times. The Lord remains faithful to us; when you finish reading everyone's chapter and story in this book, collaboration.

I Am An Overcomer; I Survived! You will know that we are all here through a divinely appointed assignment from the Lord. We can win this race with the Lord on our side always! We must always trust the process and believe that the trying of our faith worketh patience.

But let patience have her perfect work, that ye may be perfect and entirely wanting nothing.
(James 1:3-4)

Jesus said that we would have trials and tests. He also stated in his word (Peter 3:14), *"But and if ye suffer for righteousness, sake happy are ye; and be not afraid of their terror, neither be Troubled."*

God will always test us beyond measure with our faith. I want to say that steadfast in the word of God. Never allow the devil to see you sweat, no matter how challenging life may seem.

We are all champions in the Lord, to stay that we survived and came out on top! The author will share how they survived the challenging times of their lives. It was nobody, but the Lord brought us out of the fire without a smell of smoke. We are all so grateful to be alive and another chance in life. (Romans 8:31) *If God is for us, who can be against you?*

I'm hereby on a divinely appointed assignment from the Lord. I never knew that I would have to sacrifice so much of my life while doing the Lord's will. We can never say never on this journey called life. I must say that life has not been fair for me. It's all fine when everything is going fine in your life, all the bills paid, roof over your head, food in your home, and not even have to worry about being sick or shut in behind closed doors.

One day in my life, after being divorced from my second marriage for twenty-two years. I had thought my life had become 360 degrees. I was a single parent for many years. Thank God for his Grace and Mercy. I can truly say that the Lord is definitely real and always had his hand on my life as well as my Children's life. I became homeless for the first time in 2005, was on an assignment for the Lord, and was forced to stay in a shelter which was a very humble experience. I continue on my journey while working for the Lord in full-time ministry as well. I would serve the people of God, and feed through a church where I served food and meals to those that were in need as well as myself. I had been evicted and removed from my home a few times because I wasn't able to pay my rent.

There were a few times when I didn't know where I would be able to lay my head with a second child. I had experienced a life of being homeless and living some time in and out of my very own storage. I would leave the shelter to go to my job, and sometimes, I had to wash up in different restaurants and stores that were close by before I would travel to work in the morning. I was forced to live in and out of hotels and had to even sleep outdoors until daylight, and it was time to take a bus to work. I had experienced sleeping out on the bench at the beaches, bus stop, and a various times just sitting up all night outside in a chair until daylight, and I could go to my day job. I never stopped doing the work of the Lord, even through the times that I may have been homeless at least four times or more. I had to move so many times that I lost track of the times that I had been homeless.

There was a time when God would give me favor with someone who helped me out by allowing my son to stay with them for a short time until I could get on my feet and get a place of my own. I got tired of being evicted because of losing a job. Many things happened all during the times when I decided that I was going to do whatever the Lord wanted me to do. I kept on fighting with my faith, believing that trouble would not all ways. I knew that God always had a plan and purpose for my life, and that is why I never gave up on life and continued to fight the enemy, trying to take me out of there.

I always had to fight for my health for many years. I have had a major back problem ever since I had my son when I was 40 years old, and there was timing when I wasn't able to sit up and dress myself when he was seven years old. I wasn't able to walk or even stand up straight. My back had gotten even worse as I got older. I know that during the times of being homeless and there was where I had to just lay on the hard floors knowing that I had a major back problem with five Hernia disses, and Disruptor spine, and Arthritis. The doctor said that if I didn't get the surgery, I would be paralyzed from my ankle up to my waistline.

I told the doctor that I wasn't having any surgery, I was going to trust God with my back. I went down thirteen steps unconscious and didn't break any bones; that was nobody but the Lord. I was hemorrhaging with my first child in 1980, and was rushed to the hospital by the rescue. The doctor stated that the child or I wasn't going to survive; it was a 50-50 chance that I would not survive. My child was delivered when I was six months pregnant, he weighed 2 pounds 2 ounces; after five months, he died. The Lord had spared my life. In 2020, I had a stroke and didn't feel good when I woke up that morning at 7 am. I called my prayer partner and asked her to pray with me. Then I was taken to the nearest hospital for testing. I was admitted to the hospital, and the doctors stated that there was a legion on my brain the size of 4.3 centimeters.

After four days, I was discharged from the hospital with some restrictions. It was three months later, in 2021, I was called, and the doctor diagnosed me with a blood clot in my brain vessel. The only thing they could do is to monitor my brain with MRI testing every seven to eight months. God has had his hands on my life. It was not long after that I was diagnosed with an Aneurysm on my brain, then also diagnosed with Thyroid disease three months after that. I begin to say, "Lord Jesus, I don't want to hear another thing about my health anymore. I speak Isaiah 53:5."

This is why I can truly say that I Am A Overcomer. I Survived! What was meant to take me out of here? I'm still here by the grace of God. "But God, continue to keep me in the midst of what was trying to destroy me and dismiss me; the devil still didn't win. I refused to give up on the life that just made me push even hard. This also made me see that the Lord working in my life is even stronger than ever. I knew that if God had brought me through poverty, homelessness, and abandonment, I would still survive all that. Many may discourage you during this dark season of trials and storms, and you will still be walking in peace and love, and God has not taken His hands off your life. You can do even more in the kingdom of God because you know God has not given up on you. This is when you know that the hand of God is working in your favor.

There will be many that didn't believe in you and said that you would not make it through all of this. Many didn't think that you would be able to raise your child and get him or her through school and into college, but you made it through all the obstacles and challenges throughout your journey called life. We must know who we are in the Lord, and let the enemy know that we are not giving up no matter what comes or goes in life. You will have to fight to survive on this journey and fight the good fight of faith. I want to encourage you and say that quitting is never an option! The word of God says in Philippians 4:13 that I can do all things through Christ who strengtheneth me.

You have the power and the Authority to speak anything over your life. We always want to speak positively, not negatively. There may be many of you that didn't see yourself accomplishing some of your dreams and goals just over the past three years, but the favor of God has been on your life, and your latter years will be even greater and better than your past. Don't look back; keep on moving forward. It's time for you to celebrate yourself now. You owe it to yourself to give yourself a party this year in 2023. This should be your coming-out party! You can tell all your naysayers, it's your time to celebrate the Glory of God! My sister, my brother, it's time that you enjoy yourself and do you... Love yourself more now than ever before. You know that if it had not been for the Lord, who was on your side, you would not have made it to this point in life.

You have accomplished so much already in the past three years of your life, thank the Lord. God has a divine purpose and assignment and works for you to do on this journey for good. When I didn't know how I was going to feed my child and eat from day to day, not knowing where my son and I would be able to lay our heads, I continued to fight for my life and his. There were times when my child and me and to walk miles down the road, and the Lord carried the both of us. My child never missed school; he was always a hard worker in class with good grades all through school, getting honors and scholarships with the favor of God.

My son said, "Mom, everything is going to get better for us; keep the faith we are going to make it."

When a Mother has a child to encourage them to keep believing, everything will work out for us because of her faithfulness to the Lord. That encourages you even more to keep on pressing every day. Warfare has always been very intense, but having faith in the Lord will give you the perfect peace that only God can give us. Having a strong prayer life and believing in the word of God will make a great difference in your life. Storms and trials come, but you can overcome everyone with the word of God.

I want to encourage women and men if you are in your 20's, 30's, 40's, and 50's, and you may just be trying to find out your assignment and purpose on this journey. (St. Matthew 6:33) *But seek ye first the Kingdom of God, and his righteousness: and all these things shall be added unto you.*

When we spend time in his word, that will also let us know what season we are in. We want to recognize what season we are in; there is a time and a season for everything underneath the heaven. (Ecclesiastes 3:1) *To everything, there is a season and a time to every purpose under heaven.* I speak uncommon favor over your life and your household. In Jesus' Name! You shall receive more than enough, and every need in your life and your household will be meant. Focus on where you are going, not what it may look like what is going on around you right now. Surround yourself with people that want to see you succeed and reach your purpose and destiny in life. There will be people that God will put in the pathway that wants to see you excel beyond measure. God is a rewarder of them that diligently seek him. Always continue seeking God in everything, and take everything to the Lord in prayer. I know that prayer changes things and lives for the good.

My journey and Ministry have always been a faith Ministry depending on the Lord for everything, even when I didn't know how I would be able to provide and feed the two of us. I received many miracles by sowing seeds into the kingdom of God and sowing into people's life. I would give away clothes and food to the poor, and in need, many of times I would donate to shelters and give away everything if I had to relocate to another state on an assignment for the Lord. I paid a high price for the assignment on my life, and keep on fighting for my life and my children's life. (Philippians 4:19) *But my God shall supply all your need according to his riches in glory by Christ Jesus.* What helped me through challenging times in my life developing an even more, stronger prayer life, and, most of all, spending plenty of time in the word of God. That's what is going to keep us in the midst of any storm or trial that we endure on this journey called life. There are so many of us that have survived real-life challenges, but because we are still here by the Grace of God, it's not over until God says that it's over. I just want to encourage you to stay in the word of God and always have a consistent prayer life.

    Faith works if we work our faith. The devil wants us to think that God is not with us. But he is a liar. *The Lord says that I would never leave you nor forsake you.* (Psalm 31:24) Be of good courage, and he shall strengthen your heart, all ye that hope in the Lord. Believe in God's promises and know He won't let you down. Have faith in the Lord Jesus Christ, he's able to do exceedingly and abundantly, even more than what we may ask you. Nothing good comes easy. We are going to have to fight for what belongs to us and our household. (Romans 8:37) Nay in all these things we are more than a conqueror through him that loved us.

I AM AN OVERCOMER, I SURVIVED!

Contact Dr. Pastor Elaine Harvey and Speaking Events
email to
elaineharvey09@gmail.com

Dr. Elaine Harvey Live Radio & Podcast Show
www.envisionedbroadcasting.com

CEO and Founder Of Woman Of Purpose And Destiny Magazine
elaineharvey09@gmail.com

Facebook-Elaine Harvey

Instagram- Elaine Harvey

Twitter Pastor Elaine Harvey

www.elaineharvey.com

DR. ELAINE HARVEY

About Dr. Elaine Harvey

Dr. Elaine Harvey, was born and raised on June 27, 1961 in the city of South Philadelphia, PA. Pastor Graduated from Bartram High School in 1979 and shortly thereafter began studying her career journey. I attended nursing school then received my CNA License.

I attend a business school where I received a Certified Administrative Clerk Certified.

Real Estate Fundamental Course. Dr. Harvey attended the Community College in Philadelphia in Family Relations. Dr. Harvey received her BA degree Art Science at the Indiana University Of Pennsylvania college Comm Media Minor, T.V production and live Radio host broadcast since 2005.

Dr. Harvey is a Mother of two children, one daughter, and one son. She is also a Grandmother of one granddaughter. Dr. Harvey has been in the Ministry serving in her calling since 1997. Evangelizing, Witnessing, Teaching, Preaching the Gospel, Prison Ministry, and Traveling Nationwide everywhere around the world on an assignment for the Lord. Street Ministry, Women's conferences, serving the homeless in shelters all throughout many states all over the nation. She was ordained under Pastor Ethel Williams. Dr. Harvey has been Pastoring and in full-time Ministry since 2008 and is CEO and Founder of Woman of Purpose and Destiny Magazine.

CEO and Founder of her own Ministry, The Love Of Christ Ministry. Dr. Harvey Radio and Podcast Show host, T.V. Talk Show Host, Intercessor Prayer Warrior, and Nonprofit Organization. Women's Ministry, Marriage Counseling Teaching, Singles Ministry, Youth Ministry, Leadership Ministry and Teaching, and Single Couples Ministry.

DR. ELAINE HARVEY

Graphic designer, Self-Publisher, Author of several books, Bestseller of I Am A Survivor Autobiography was Published in 2008. Her second book is Victory Over Your Enemies, God Favored Me, Anthology, released in December 2022, 2X Best Seller, & #1 Best Seller International in Australia, Don't Give Up On Love! These books are listed on Amazon.com and Barnes and Noble.com. My fifth book Anthology Collaboration will be released in February 2023, "I Am A Overcomer, I Survived!"

You can follow me on Facebook live every Sunday afternoon at 3 PM EST, where I preach and teach the word of God. Facebook live on The Power Of Prayer on Mon & Wed @ 8:30 PM EST
Follow me on Instagram under Elaine Harvey
Twitter under Elaine Harvey
You can email me for live speaking and events
elaineharvey09@gmail.com

Be *Fierce*, For You Are Destined To Overcome.
By Dr. Deborah Allen

It was destined - Developing according to a plan, certain to meet (a particular fate), intended for or traveling toward (a specific place).

Hear the inspiring call to every warrior of God, for this anthology, is written and birthed by fire through my very existence. As I pen and get this anthology ready to be published, I have lived through one of the greatest testimonies of my entire life. This path of my life has been fierce in this dispensation. Yet, "I am an overcomer!"

Truly comprehend and recognize that we are destined. It has been predestined by the hand and mind of God that we would be born even made to be fierce! People of God, we are destined for greatness. Appreciate that fierceness resides in each of us. God destines us for this intense, royal battle called life. We have been orchestrated in the plan of our amazing God. Our life is our road map to our destiny. As I have aged, wisdom has been such a gift for me to see that our steps are truly ordered. God designed a purpose for each one of us. My existence is not a mistake but a blessing. God has always had me in his mind, even before the foundation of the world. I was not planning, but I am not a mishap. I was so destined to be here that God knows the very hairs on my head. I know the enemy has told us all our lives that we are mistakes. The enemy and even people have said you are a waste of space. The devil has belittled and mocked us. However, that's all but a lie from the pit. We are destined, loved, chosen, wonderfully, and fearfully made. Even how we look, walk, talk, weigh, height, hair, and color are predestined. Our lives are so valuable that God mapped them out just for us. Our God took thought for our lives, planned for us, and set it all up for us to win. You are the apple of God's eye, and his favor rests upon us. We're so very loved. My existence, trials, hurts, setbacks, defeats, falls, disappointments, failures, stumbles, and victories are all in the plan of God. My life is written by the very hand of God. From being a preemie baby, molested as a child, teenage mother, suicidal wife, battered woman, divorcee, single, business owner, and Pastor, have all been destined and planned by God just for me.

    How amazing that my life is not a surprise to God and our God knows how to perform all things well. Every life experience has been used to build, make, purify, mold, shape, and refine me. It all works according to God's vision. Rest assured that destiny has been in and at play in our lives. Our lives are not just thrown together as an afterthought. No, our lives are not chaotic messes. Destiny is before me and calls to me. "The steps of a good man are ordered by the LORD" (Ps. 37:23). My steps are ordered and mapped out clearly. God always planned for me to be victorious and be an over-comer. God destined me to win. We are born to win. Rest assured, you will accomplish the course of your life. God has a reason for us being alive. Our very fate is in the hand of our Savior. We can trust the all-knowing God with our lives. We belong to God and are his. The devil does not own us, for we are God's children. God is a faultless architect in this amazing and flawless plan of life.

Fierce--Having or displaying an intense or ferocious aggressiveness, violent in force and intensity. "And from the days of John the Baptist until now the kingdom of heaven suffereth violence, and the violent take it by force" (Matt. 11:12). Ding, ding, ding! That's the bell, and the battle has started for the people of God. Let's take up and fiercely fight against everything that is fighting us. Let's arm ourselves to rage war. Fiercely go to battle and subdue every kingdom, salutation, or problem in your way. I mean utterly, destroy all the spiritual wickedness in high places. Let us be victorious and even snatch it by force. When I think of fierce, I think of tenacity, strength, endurance, and power. We must overcome all the attacks of the devil. Brawl, slash, kick, shed blood, struggle, and pursue victory.

Fierce makes me think of being in the military and defending ourselves at all costs. We are born gladiators. Gladiators can fight to the death against animals, even vicious attacks. Gladiators were made to be strong and invincible. They know to combat and truly fight for their lives. Remember, as the body of God, we are the defenders of the faith. Fierce is what God designed us to be. We are created in the image of a great, even terrible, God. We're designed and fashioned to last time, trials, and tribulations. You are different (sanctified) from everyone else. God is a ferocious God, and he's breathed fierceness into us. Please watch the company we keep, for it determines our mindset.

Our environment does play a part in our lives. Who we have fellowship with has a significant impact on us. Our association with other people influences us. Understand that we need to and must connect with strong people of purpose. We don't want to be connected to weak people or people who have no strength. Do not surround yourself with fearful or doubt-having folks. Fearful people will corrupt and pollute the entire camp. Scared people impute into our spirits stinking thinking and fearful words and thoughts. They speak only of defeat, even doubt. They are plain old scared. They are already defeated in their minds and can't even see the victory yet to come. We need people on our side, people that have our backs. I mean that it's important to build with that right tribe than when you are fighting, you know they are fighting too.

      Through this passage of life, we must press forward and continue to war and fight the good fight of faith. "Fight the good fight of faith, lay hold on eternal life, whereunto thou art also called, and hast professed a good profession before many witnesses" 1 Tim. 6:12. We are witnesses to the fact that God is a deliverer. Our lives are living testimony that is being seen and read by others. I have been through some trying times, yet those times caused me to "become" who God purposed me to be from the beginning. We've had to carry our crosses while walking with Christ. "Behold, I give unto you power to tread on serpents and scorpions, and over all the power of the enemy: and nothing shall by any means hurt you" Luke 10:19. It took me a long time to understand this powerful truth. Glory to God! It made me fight, endure, go through, and win. It was always in my mind and heart to be great and be a world changer, but there was a time I struggled with this. About five years ago, I went through a stripping in my life that I thought was going to kill me! Remarkably the process allowed me to become her to be her. That meant I had to live through that time to become the best version of myself, and I reinvented myself. That season was a time of looking in my hand to see what I had to be great again. I had to do the most challenging thing ever: get up again. Not only did I have to get up, but also, I had to dream again. It was a season of purging, shifting, and self-growth. God rebuilt me to become better for the kingdom and destiny. God is rebuilding you as well. He is restoring you, and you will have a greater purpose and even stronger anointing upon your life. You are better equipped now to battle like never before. Not only that, God has made us better to focus and to lead. It's now your season and moment, so believe in yourself again. Glory to God; it's the time to reach for and acquire the blessings of the Lord. After that, my God, my God, is all I can say! All we must do is fight to win. Our families will be victorious. Our friends will be too. Yes, even our ministries will be elevated. Everything attached to us wins! We must be strong. We must stand God and be fierce, for we have overcome!

I AM AN OVERCOMER, I SURVIVED!

THE FIERCE SYSTEM:

F – Find yourself...Find your true self and be true to your voice, dreams, and goals.

I – Indeed, be independent... Indeed be independent, for you are the difference maker in your life and the entire world.

E- Evaluate your life & story... Evaluate your story and life from clear eyes, not the eyes of your past and unlearned you.

R – Realize you make a difference... Realize life is better because you are here and have a purpose of fulfilling.

C – Create opportunity through purpose... Create opportunity through purpose, the gift in your hand that will bring you before great men and allows you to make wealth.

E – Evolve into the greatest version of you... Evolve into the greatest version of you that the process of time has allowed you to become who you were born to be.

*** I have a gift for you:
https://deborahallen.groovepages.com/free/index ***
SIGNATURE PROGRAM LINK
https://sites.google.com/view/executive-firce-coaching/home

Acknowledgements

Writing will forever be the tool that allowed me to reinvent myself! Also, being an author has brought my authentic voice back into my life and the lives of many on a global scale. I'm grateful for all the support and love that has graciously shown me throughout the years. Kudos and a special thanks to Fierce Tv (viewers) and The Fierce, Ignition & Activation Show/Podcast (listeners). Please know I am forever grateful!

I serve in ministry with a mighty man of valor, Apostle Dr. Glen Allen Sr, who has embraced the fierceness in me. Lighthouse Apostolic Ministries of God Church "The House of The Prophets" a sincere thank you for always being a place of advancement, change, purpose, vision, love, and even dreams.

Wondrously, I have birthed six children, but I'm the mother of nine. Our children have been a blessing to my very existence. I'm so awed by my support from family, friends, and clients. All your love has been priceless. You have been the "why" inside of me!

"When walking in purpose, fiercely walk in divine authority."
-Apostle Dr. Deborah Allen

I AM AN OVERCOMER, I SURVIVED!

About - Dr. Deborah Allen

Finding one's *inner voice* can be a liberating, awe-inspiring, and transformational experience.

Fashioned to help the masses find their "fierce"; is the dynamic professional Deborah Allen.

Deborah Allen is a 25X best-selling & 12X international best-selling author, speaker, certified life coach, cleric, and CEO and creative founder of **The Fierce System**, a multifaceted liaison specialty, centered around helping women to both, find and develop their voice. Having been trained by world-renowned NSA motivational speaker Mr. Les Brown, Deborah understands the importance of strategy, development, and credible mentorship, traits she seamlessly translates to her growing clientele.

Deborah's mantra is simple: Her only goal is to motivate clients, helping them to create the life they were meant to live.

Refusing mediocrity on all fronts, Deborah has trailblazed a credible path for those she serves. She has served as Senior Pastor of Lighthouse Apostolic Ministries of God Church for the last 23 years; and is the Executive Director of the nonprofit organization L.A.M. Ministries, Inc.

Matching servant leadership with incredible respect for higher learning, Deborah is a Certified Life Coach, a member of the National Speaker Association Speaker (NSA), and a Black Speakers Network (BSN) Speaker. Her conglomerate, The Fierce System, comprises many platforms, including Fierce TV, Radio, and blog; as well as Fierce Voices of Destiny Program; where she mentors, develops, and creates strategic alignment between clients and their true life's calling. She is the Visionary and CEO of Igniting The Flame Publishing, Visionary Coaching & Consulting Group LLC, and Deborah Allen Enterprise.

Deborah proudly attests that women are at the heartbeat of all she does and that it is her desire to see them be strong and fierce and know that they can truly achieve their dreams and walk in purpose. When she is not helping women come alive, rebuild, shift and find themselves again, Deborah is a valued asset to her communal body and a loving member of her family and friendship circles.

Dr. Deborah Allen. Energizer. Organizer. Servant Leader.

DR. DEBORAH ALLEN

Contact Information:
Apostle/Ambassador Dr. Deborah Allen
www.deborahallenfierce.com
www.ignitingtheflamepublishing.com
Email: deborahallenfierce@gmail.com

Links:

Facebook: https://www.facebook.com/deborahallenfierce

Instagram: https://www.instagram.com/deborahallenfierce/

Twitter: https://twitter.com/deborahallenfie

YouTube: https://www.youtube.com/channel/UCTOf0igcAxlVaneH2ZOo_Zg

2nd Website: https://deborahallenspeaker.com/

You Can Overcome Too
By Ivy Caldwell

We all have been given the opportunity at life and to live to the best of our ability. Sometimes, no matter what we do, our lives just seem not to work out the way we planned them or the way we thought they should go. We can never get past the life experiences that have weighed us down emotionally. Life has a way of throwing some terrible things our way; no matter what it is, you can overcome it too.

What does it mean to overcome? According to Merriam-Webster's Dictionary, it means the following:

1. "(tr) to get the better of in a conflict. 2. (tr; often passive) to render incapable or powerless by laughter, sorrow, exhaustion, etc.: he was overcome by fumes. 3. (tr) to surmount (obstacles, objections, etc.)
2. The definition of *overcome is t* 1: to get the better of: surmount overcome difficulties They *overcame* the enemy. 2: overwhelm were overcome by the heat and smoke: to gain the

superiority: win strong in the faith, that truth would overcome"[1]

According to Microsoft Bing, it means the following: "succeed in dealing with (a problem or difficulty): defeat (an opponent); prevail: (of an emotion) overpower or overwhelm."[2]

I am an overcomer! Are you an overcomer? What have you overcome? What are you contemplating battling right now? What are you in the middle of right now? What is hindering you from taking a leap of faith to get to the other side of that thing that stops you in your tracks? You may not be where you want to be, but you are an overcomer too. You are still here to tell your story! This is a part of your journey, and you will get through this. You wait and see how God will show Himself strong on your behalf.

All of our life experiences, the pain, the trauma, the misunderstandings, the neglect, the betrayal, the confusion, the abandonment, the rejection, the toxic

---

[1] https://www.merriam-webster.com/dictionary/overcome

[2] https://www.bing.com/search?FORM=AFSCWO&PC=AFSC&q=overcome

relationships, the missed opportunities, job loss, health issues, family drama, bankruptcy, loss of a loved one or multiple losses, the divorce, the defeat and the overwhelm of it all. You have come to a place and wonder how in the world I will make it through this. What am I to do with what I am faced with today? How am I going to do this? How do I go on? Is living worth it? Where do I go from here? All these questions are valid, and you will get your answers in time. Your pain is real; it's a deep wound, and don't you dare stifle it. If you need to cry, let the tears flow. If you need to yell it out, shout the walls down like you are at Jericho's Wall. Don't throw anything because you will have to clean it up and buy another one. Laughter is good for your soul, and I know it's painful but don't lose your sense of humor. Your anger is warranted, but don't let it cause you to sin.

First things first, breathe and catch your breath. **Second**, access the situation. **Third**, weigh your options. **Fourth**, talk to God about it. **Fifth**, get yourself some support because you are going to need it. Don't do this on your own. Don't let pride stop you from seeking help. God created us to be in communion with others, even through hard times. **Sixth**, find appropriate Scriptures to meditate on, memorize, pray, and speak them over your life and situation. **Seventh**, it's time to get a game plan in place. You will overcome this! You will survive this! No matter what it looks like and no matter what, it feels like it's not over.

When we are going through life experiences, we ask ourselves, "Why is this happening to me?"

I don't know, but God knows exactly what He is doing and does not make mistakes. Talk to Him while you are going through this. God will walk you through this. You will overcome this too! I know the situation does not look good; quite frankly, being in this place is just downright scary. You didn't see this coming and didn't expect it at all. God is not taken by surprise by anything that we go through. I know you are afraid but don't let fear set in; steady yourself and keep the pace. You are on schedule according to God's plan in your life's journey. God knew this was going to happen, my dear. God has sanctioned you to be in this place at this juncture in your life. There is an overcomer deep down on the inside of you, and you will have to pull it up. God has His hand upon you, and you are His child. God has great plans in store for you. I know it's cloudy now, and you can't see your way, but you are born of God.

(I John 5:4 NKJV) "For whatever is born of God overcomes the world. And this is the victory that has *overcome* the world—our faith."

If you are saved and belong to God, you have what you need inside you to overcome it. You have the power of God living inside you, and it's time for you to use what God has given you." You have the creator living inside you, and it's time for you to take hold of the power within you. This is just a test, and you will overcome it. This is a test that you will pass with flying colors. You will not let this push you back to how you used to be. You are not going to lash out at others. You are not going to fight back in the flesh. Why?

Because we "Do not be *overcome* by evil but *overcome* evil with good." (Romans 12:21 NKJV) We all have been mistreated in one way or another in this life and have been tempted to get even. We have been tempted to take matters into our own hands. We have been consumed with anger because of our experiences; we let that spirit take control and yield to it. We have made matters worse because we didn't let God handle the situation.

God lets us know that "Beloved, do not avenge yourselves, but rather give place to wrath; for it is written, *Vengeance* is Mine, I will repay," says the Lord. (Romans 12:19 NKJV)

If we take matters into our own hands, we will make a mess. It may feel good to the flesh for a moment, but you will have regret afterward. You don't want to stay in this place longer than you must, so wait for the Lord to avenge you. God does not need our help, and God got you. Don't worry about a thing because God will take care of evil-doers. God will prepare a table before you in the presence of your enemies. While God is doing what He has to do, it's time for you to do what you must do. You have to mind your heart, your mind, and your mouth.

Don't let your heart become hardened; cast down those thoughts that are not of God and use your mouth to confess God's word over your situation. Speak those things that are not as though they were, and you wait for them to manifest. It's time to open your mouth and praise God through the storm. Now is the time to worship God and draw close to Him.

"And they overcame him *by the blood of the* Lamb and *by the* word *of* their testimony, and they did not love their lives to *the* death." Revelation 12:11 (NKJF)

God has given us the power and authority to dominate the earth. How do we do this? It's in our mouths; God spoke the world into existence and expected us to shape our worlds. Through our testimony, we overcame the situation and experienced hurt, betrayal, misunderstanding, abuse, and word curses. There is freedom in telling your testimony. Think about it; we have all that steam, vapor, or breath locked down inside us, and we tend to hold on to it instead of letting it go. It's time to speak it! Go ahead a testify of the goodness of the Lord.

The enemy thought that experience would take you out of here and stop you. But you are here today because of God's grace and mercy. You are stronger because of it. You are better because of it. You are wiser because of it. Go ahead and give God praise! Hallelujah, and thank you, Jesus! I am still here, and there is a purpose deep down inside me that is getting ready to be birthed. You are getting ready to inspire many lives with your testimony. You are getting ready to be an encouragement to those who don't see a way out. You are getting ready to see a breakthrough in your life! Are you ready for your breakthrough? You are going to have to expose your truth! That's right; you will have to talk about whatever is ailing you.

Although you might be overcome with grief, pain, and no hope, there is nothing that you can't overcome.

God has said in His word, "No temptation has overtaken you except such as is common to man; but God is faithful, who will not allow you to be tempted beyond what you are able, but with the temptation will also make the way of escape, that you may be able to bear it." (I Corinthians 10:13 NKJV)

God is faithful, and you may be in a season of bewilderment, but all seasons change. Get ready because your change is on the way. God knew you could handle this; look to Him for your escape as you bear it. God will take you through this season to get to the next one. You are at the break of the day! Baby, the Son is getting ready to shine upon you, never like before. You are not defeated; you are an overcomer and have prevailed in the situation. Lift up your head and see the salvation of the Lord.

"Yet in all these things *we* are *more than* conquerors through Him who loved *us*." (Romans 8:37 NKJV) In all that you go through, you are a conqueror because God says so.

It's time for you to affirm yourself! Get in front of a mirror and repeat these words daily until you feel them. Say them until they become the essence of who you are because you believe them.

- This is the beginning of a new chapter in my life!
- I will do what I have to do to heal from this!
- My story is not over, and I am right on track!
- I will survive this!
- I will ask for help!
- I will overcome this!
- God will use this for His glory!
- I will trust the process!
- I will survive this too!

God will redeem the time. God will give you beauty for your ashes. God will be the lifter up of your head. God will restore the joy of your salvation. God will give you peace that surpasses your understanding.

I am a living witness that God will restore your soul if you let Him! The joy of the Lord is your strength. If God did it for me, He will do it for you too! You can overcome too, and don't you ever forget it.

IVY CALDWELL

About - Ivy Caldwell

Ivy Caldwell is an ordained elder, wife, mom, grandmother, 15X Author, 6X Bestseller, and TV &

Podcast host. She is located in upstate New York. She is a transformation life coach urging women to "**Step Into ANEW You,**" declaring, "It is time for women to reclaim their voice, power, authority, life, and joy back." *No longer sit in mute agreement with fear, hurt, anguish and humiliation; look the elephant in the room directly in the eyes and Expose It!* God has given her this assignment, and she is tenacious and determined to deliver hope and healing to the wounded.

    It's time to break free from years of emotional baggage. She admits that she, too, is an overcomer of abuse and that it took her years to finally be at peace and be liberated. A highly driven woman born to break barriers, she proves that when powered by purpose, you can become unstoppable. Today she personifies what it means to ascend above adversity while inspiring countless others to do the same. Extraordinary at walking others through a radical transformation, she is as relentless about her client's success as her own. She is more than their coach. She's their champion and shows them how to overcome.

    Expose It! Let Your Healing Process Begin is a book with a companion workbook that aims to support readers in starting their emotional healing process. *Begin today by "**Stepping Into ANEW You**" by confronting your past trauma.* It's time to release and let it go. **Expose It**!

IVY CALDWELL

To inquire about her books, coaching programs, tv, and podcast shows, or to schedule her for a public appearance, book signing, or speaking engagement, contact her at ivy@footprintenterprisesllc.com or connect with her at the following social media outlets:

Facebook:
https://www.facebook.com/ivy.caldwell.718
Facebook Author Page:
https://www.facebook.com/112368728147813
Instagram:
https://www.instagram.com/footprintseries
LinkedIn: https://www.linkedin.com/in/ivy-caldwell-94612441
YouTube: YouTube: YouTube.com/@ivycaldwell
Website: https://footprintenterprisesllc.com
TV Show: https://rethinktv.life/browse/

Podcast: https://anchor.fm/ivy-caldwell

Etsy Shop:
https://www.etsy.com/shop/ANEWYouDesigns?ref=seller-platform-mcnav

I AM AN OVERCOMER, I SURVIVED!

Woman Behind The Mask By Dr. Elizabeth Perkins

When you finally decide to take off your mask, it will feel like removing layers of dead skin you have carried around with you for years. Therefore, after removing your mask, which represents the pains from your past, you will be able to do what you have desired to do the most: breathe again, live again and move again into your destiny.

As I took off my mask, I could feel the pains from my past lifting from my soul. However, it was not easy, nor was it meant to be. The days, the months, and the years went by as the Lord operated and placed me on His table to be healed. Not only was I being healed, but I was also being set free. There were times when the intensity of the pain seemed overwhelming. I spent many days and nights all alone, removing the pains of my past and the residue attached to my soul. While I wrote about this journey, I felt the bandages I used to cover up everything slowly, gently, and strategically peeled away by the Lord himself.

He was the chief surgeon. I was the patient. With love, purpose, and compassion, the Lord took off the mask I wore for years as my protection. "For he saith to Moses, I will have mercy on whom I will have mercy, and I will have compassion on whom I will have compassion. So then it is not of him that willeth, or of him that runneth, but of God that showeth mercy," according to the scripture in Romans 9:15-16. The Lord had mercy on me, cleansed my wounds, and healed me from the pains of my past.

After the Lord gave me His grace and mercy, I learned to breathe again. Breathe again represents the capacity to exhale the old and inhale the new. When these two are done simultaneously, you will breathe again freely without wearing a mask. From this explanation of my testimony, I recognized that the ability to breathe again gives a renewal and a refreshing of the soul and renders a new start for life. "And the Lord God formed man of the dust of the ground and breathed into his nostrils the breath of life, and man became a living soul," according to the book of Genesis 2:7. Breath also means to inhale air into the lungs, and expel it. It also means to inhale, to exhale, and most importantly, to live. The purpose and the understanding of breathing are just as valid and important as – life. If breathing is absent, then so is life.

Hence, when these two ingredients are not mixed and combined, the equation that is reached is only a mere existence of something and not real life or living. For that reason, breathing not only gives a person the ability to live, but it also provides an internal strength and a sound that ignites the soul to live again. Thus, I had to breathe again to process my hurts, deal with the pains of my past and walk into my healing. Initially, breathing again was harder than I thought. It required letting go of those things that were suffocating my soul. However, I had to breathe if I truly wanted to live again. I did just that!

Before I moved into the newness God had for my life, I had to release my testimony that lingered in my heart for years. I recognized my past experiences, and the memories I constantly rehearsed in my mind almost crippled me. I am so grateful I obeyed the Lord and wrote my testimony. Based on the word, *"This is the disciple which testifieth of these things, and wrote these things: and we know that his testimony is true."* (John 21:24)

I was forced to leave the dry places in my life, which represented gloominess, abuse, sadness, emptiness, dark clouds, frustration, brokenness, low self-esteem, and loneliness. As much as I desperately wanted to walk into the new, I could not walk into the fullness of what God wanted until I unloaded the pains and the history of my past. Some of the experiences were awful and almost grave. God used the darkest and ugliest moments in my life to give

Him – glory. As declared in the book of Revelation, *"Thou art worthy, O Lord, to receive glory and honor and power: for thou hast created all things, and for thy pleasure, they are and were created."* (Revelation 4:11)

    I never thought I would have had the courage to face everything I went through, from a young child to a woman. Nevertheless, I discovered it was not my strength that carried me. It was the strength of the Lord, the love, the mercy, the grace of Jesus Christ, and the power of the Holy Spirit. I could not have completed this work of deliverance on my own. I could not have left the pains of my past behind without the help of my – Lord. Because of this, I have humbled my will even more.

    For many years, I was exhausted from privately and quietly living behind the mask I had worn for years. As I carved out the words and the pages for this book, I realized I had lived this way for years. Yet, I only discovered this because I faced those things I struggled with for years, those that terrified me the most, and those I hid. "And, when the woman saw that she was not hiding, she came trembling, and falling before him, she declared unto him before all the people for what cause she had touched him, and how she was immediately healed. And, he said unto her, Daughter, be of good cheer: thy faith hath made thee whole, go in peace," according to the book of Luke 8:47.

I was like this woman. I had so many issues. I needed to be healed. Nevertheless, my healing was not easy. It was not even wanted. Yet, I needed to live again. It was essential for me to be a new woman again. I suffered from the memories long enough. As the Apostle Peter wrote in the word of God, *"But the God of all grace, who hath called us unto his eternal glory by Christ Jesus, after that ye have suffered a while, make you perfect, stablish, strengthen, and settle you."* (I Peter 5:10) With assurance and gratefulness, I celebrate the restoration of my soul and the newness the Lord has allowed to come my way.

With this being said, I am so humbled that the Lord allowed me to stay right where I was until I removed the mask, which kept my life internally and externally at a standstill. The healing which took place on His surgical table cannot be replaced. This was how the Lord chose for me to be healed properly and thoroughly, despite what I wanted. Moreover, my tears of joy cannot be fully explained on paper. Only my Father in heaven knows how this book saved my mind, brought my soul out of darkness, and released me from the pains of my past.

You can remove the mask you have secretly worn and privately lived behind for years. I will not say that removing your mask will be the easiest thing to do, but it is one of the greatest accomplishments you can ever achieve. As the bible has declared, *"All things are possible to those who believe."* God has given you the power and the authority to take off the mask that has stolen our joy, your peace, and even our purpose.

God has given you the power to remove the mask which has caused your life to seem limited and your purpose to be placed on hold. When you have worn a mask, which has caused you to live behind your private pains and hidden hurts for a large part of your life, you t lived the life God designed for you. No matter how much your life has seemed prosperous and possibly even blessed, you truly have not seen and received the best God has until you have allowed God to walk with you and assist you so that you can live without a mask.

I want to encourage every man and woman to remove the mask that has held them captive as prisoners of their past. No matter what you have gone through, I want you to be honest with the Lord about the things which have caused you pain and grief and come out from living behind your mask. I want to encourage you to breathe again. I want to encourage you to be the new man or woman God called you to be. Lastly, I want to encourage you to live your life. However, I want to admonish you to live without living behind a MASK.

I AM AN OVERCOMER, I SURVIVED!

About - Dr. Elizabeth Perkins

Dr. Elizabeth Perkins is the founder of Elizabeth Perkins Global Ministries and Resurrection Global Ministries. She walks in an Apostolic,

Prophetic, and Evangelistic Anointing. She has preached the Gospel in the U.S. and Internationally. She has traveled to Nigeria, where she preached the Word of God in Benin City, Wari, Sapele in Delta State, and other villages.

Dr. Perkins is an Author, Poet, and Publisher of Deliverance For The Soul Publishing House, where she houses her poetry and books. She is the author of Excess Baggage, Woman Behind The Mask, The Fight Of My Life, Woman Of Many Nations, and Her soon new release Man Of Many Nations.

She is also the Founder of the Excess Baggage Conference, The Fight Of My Life Conference, and the Creator of Her Annual Woman Behind The Mask Conference, birthed and designed to heal women from the pains of their past.

In her Professional Career, she serves and works as an Elementary School Teacher. Furthermore, she has worked in runaway homes for girls and boys and transitional living centers for youth in Tulsa, Oklahoma. As a result of her passion for Education, she recently launched Elizabeth University, An Educational Training School For Boys and Girls where she provides classes and seminars.

Dr. Elizabeth Perkins is a native of Orange, Texas. However, she has lived in various states. She served eight years in the United States Naval Reserves. She received her Bachelor Of Arts In Political Science and English from Prairie View A & M University and her Master's Degree In Theology and Missions from Oral Roberts University in Tulsa, Oklahoma.

As an Intercessor and a Prayer Warrior, Dr. Perkin's messages of truth, encouragement, and deliverance have touched the lives of people who have struggled with pains from their past, such as abandonment, depression, low self-esteem, suicide, and other inward scars.

Dr. Elizabeth Perkins is a woman who is submitted to the will of the LORD. Her ministry manifests compassion for the lost, troubled souls, the forgotten, and healing, deliverance, and miracles. She is convinced that her ministry is to free the captives and release them into their destiny.

To Contact Dr. Elizabeth Perkins:

Dr. Elizabeth Perkins Global Ministries:
1.800.965.1664

Social Media:
Elizabeth Perkins/Facebook
Dr. Elizabeth Perkins/Facebook

Overcoming Difficult Situations
By Taletha Morrison

How do we overcome difficult situations? Maybe you've asked yourself this question many times. Sometimes the road to overcoming difficult situations seems long and tedious, but once you learn key strategies, you will be victorious. You must begin to trust God in a way you've never trusted Him before. When you develop a track record with God, you will trust Him in every situation. He will always come through and never fail you. He is faithful to His word. We must be mentally tough and fully persuaded that God is faithful to His promises. So, testify of His goodness.

The book of Revelations, chapters 11 and 12, says that we are overcome by the blood of the lamb and the word of our testimony. That tells us that when Jesus died on the cross, He was the lamb slain for all mankind. So, we have victory in every area of our lives. We must testify to these accounts. When Jesus healed the man with leprosy, only one came back to testify about being made whole. We must always keep our faith in action and walk in our authority. Just like

Abraham being fully persuaded to walk in the oneness with God, he overcame difficult situations. And, if you spend time with God, He will help you overcome the trials in your life. Meditating, reading the word, and seeking God's face daily will allow you to hear from God.

When you pray, God will speak to you through His word. He wants you to dedicate prayer time to Him, and the Holy Spirit will lead and guide you into all truth. Often, we are looking for our situations to change quickly. However, we have to be willing to let God direct our path. When the enemy tries to attack your mind with doubt and unbelief, you must cast that doubt down and put faith there. We defeat the enemy by standing on the Word of God and having a heart of forgiveness. We have to forgive those who try to use us or mishandle us. The Bible tells us that we don't wrestle against flesh and blood but against principalities and spiritual wickedness in high places. This is spiritual warfare, and we must equip ourselves with God. We want the love of God to be so deep in our lives that nothing can destroy it.

God called us to do an assignment and not to be distracted by the devices of this world. Our worship will draw us closer to God. It will be like a sweet perfume in His nostrils. And, our gealing and peace in His word. He will deliver us from all the evil forces in our lives. God will allow us to overcome and restore us to a place of blessings and prosperity. While restoration takes place, we must remain faithful to Him and not allow the enemy to deceive us. It is important to put away idols and evaluate our walk with Him.

God is revealing and demonstrating signs the s, miracles, and wonders for us to see. All He requires from us is to be obedient and trust Him in every required life. All you have to do is believe and apply more faith to your life. It is time to walk in your freedom and the power God has given you.

Acknowledgements

Special thanks to Dr. Elaine Harvey for the opportunity to participate in this anthology and for being a blessing to the body of Christ. I believe many will find freedom and a renewed spirit as they read this wonderful collaboration. This was orchestrated by the Holy Spirit, and I am truly grateful. I would like to acknowledge my children, who have kept me going. Thank you to Cassandra Lane. May God continue to bless you richly.

Contact Information

Facebook
Taletha Morrison

Instagram
Pretty.for.a.day

YouTube
Taletha Morrison

I AM AN OVERCOMER, I SURVIVED!

About - Taletha Morrison

Prophetess Taletha would be the first to say, as the apostle Paul wrote in 1 Corinthians 11, that one imitates her as she imitates Christ. There have been many aspirations and diligent laborers of Godly women before her within 20 centuries of ministry, And to them, she is truly grateful for being obedient to God allow him to open the door for other ministries to have a platform. Her walk with God has been a commitment of choice. Lady Taletha is a woman of power, love, and compassion it hasn't always been this way. She suffered from depression, feeling worthless and anxiety, Squiggling to be free and didn't know how But God opened the door set her free now she is flourishing in the things of God, Helping to push others to their next level and she continues to Walk in her God-given purpose for her life she is a very proud mother of two, a grandmother of two, she loves life, as well as she, loves ministry.

A Great Work: Finishing Strong with No More Spiritual Miscarriage
By Ricky James Allen-Callahan

Sanballat, Tobiah, Geshem the Arab, and the rest of our enemies found out that I had finished rebuilding the wall and that no gaps remained—though we had not yet set up the doors in the gates. So Sanballat and Geshem sent a message asking me to meet them at one of the villages in the plain of Ono. But I realized they were plotting to harm me, so I replied by sending this message to them: "I am engaged in great work, so I can't come. Why should I stop working to come and meet with you?" Four times they sent the same message, and each time I gave the same reply. Nehemiah 6:1-4 NLT

1. Stay on the Wall

Don't get drawn into debate when you are doing something great. You will never reach your destination if you stop and throw rocks at every dog that barks. Winston Churchill.

I am saying this for your benefit, not to place restrictions on you. I want you to do whatever will help you serve the Lord best, with as few distractions as possible. I Corinthians 7:35 NLT. Continued the work with even greater Determination.

The fifth time, Sanballat's servant came with an open letter in his hand, and this is what it said, "There is a rumor among the surrounding nations, and Geshem tells me it is true, that you and the Jews are planning to rebel, and that is why you are building the wall. According to his reports, you plan to be their king. He also reports that you have appointed prophets in Jerusalem to proclaim about you, Look! There is a king in Judah! You can be sure that this report will get back to the king, so I suggest you come and talk it over with me."

I replied, "There is no truth in any part of your story. You are making up the whole thing." They were trying to intimidate us, imagining they could discourage and stop the work. So I continued the work with even greater determination. Nehemiah 6:5-9 NLT. Double down on your commitment. A Lie has speed. Truth has Endurance.

Take with me your share of hardship [passing through the difficulties you are called to endure] like a good soldier of Christ Jesus. No soldier in active service gets entangled in the [ordinary business] affairs of civilian life; [he avoids them] so that he may please the one who enlisted him to serve. And if anyone competes as an athlete [in competitive games], he is not crowned [with the wreath of victory] unless he competes according to the rules. The hard-working farmer [who labors to produce crops] ought to be the first to receive his share of the crops. Think over the things I am saying [grasp their application], for the Lord will grant you insight and understanding. II Timothy 2:3-7 AMP

And now, dear brothers and sisters, one final thing. Fix your thoughts on what is true, and honorable, and right, and pure, lovely, and admirable. Think about things that are excellent and worthy of praise. Philippians 4:8 NLT

So, on October 2nd, the wall was finished—just fifty-two days after we had begun. When our enemies and the surrounding nations heard about it, they were frightened and humiliated. They realized this work had been done with the help of our God. Nehemiah 6:15-16 NLT. You are never without Help (The Person of Jesus Christ.) Help from The Helper (The Person of the Holy Spirit.) After the wall was finished and I had set up the doors in the gates, the gatekeepers, singers, and Levites were appointed.

I gave the responsibility of governing Jerusalem to my brother Hanani, along with Hananiah, the commander of the fortress, for he was a faithful man who feared God more than most. Nehemiah 7:1-2 NLT. Don't be afraid to give Power Away. Kingdom People give it when you give it away. It Multiplies + "Demonstration."

The lighting of candles, if we can, Then we Must!

I again saw under the sun that the race is not to the swift and the battle is not to the strong, and neither is bread to the wise nor riches to those of intelligence and understanding nor favor to men of ability, but time and chance overtake them all. Ecclesiastes 9:11 AMP Four Nuggets:

1. Keep your Heart Postured in Humility.

2. Live Life in the Realm of the Spirit, Not in the Realm of the Flesh and Carnal Thinking.

3. Stay focused! Watch out for those Distractions!

4. Always Let Love be shed abroad in your Heart

" No More Spiritual Miscarriages "

Psalm 119:28 says, My soul weeps because of grief; strengthen me according to Your word. For if He causes grief, then He will have compassion, according to His abundant lovingkindness. Lamentations 3:32, NASB

Be strong and let your heart take courage, all you who hope in the LORD. Psalm 31:24, NASB
Our hope for you is unshaken, for we know that as you share in our sufferings, you will also share in our comfort. II Corinthians 1:7, ESV

"Here on earth you will have many trials and sorrows; but cheer up, for I (Jesus) have overcome the world. ," John 16:33, TLB

You made all the delicate inner parts of my body and knit them together in my mother's womb. Psalm 139:13, ESV

Now may the God of hope fill you with all joy and peace in believing so that you will abound in hope by the power of the Holy Spirit. Romans 15:13, NASB

Pregnancy after loss means there are no guarantees. You know now that babies can die. This is a terrible truth to learn. You no longer assume anything about how your or your child's life will turn out. Spiritually? The challenge is to trust. You may be angry at God. You might feel like God has betrayed you. You may not be sure what you believe anymore.

It is hard to trust that this journey will end well. But trust is not a one-time decision to be made. You're learning to believe in your body, life, and God in new ways. It's never easy, but you are not alone. "It is the Lord who goes before you. He will be with you; he will not fail you or forsake you. Do not fear or be dismayed." Deuteronomy 31:8

For me, the companionship of God is the only thing I can trust right now. I don't know what will happen next. I only know that God has been with me in the past, is here in the present, and will be with me in the future. For now, that is enough. Pregnancy after loss brings a daily temptation to despair. When you know the worst that can happen, it's hard to stop thinking it could happen again. You're always holding your breath, waiting for the other shoe to drop. Despair thrives under perfect conditions like these. Spiritually? The challenge is to hope.

You may hate well-meaning comments that everything will turn out right this time. You might hold off preparing for the baby because you don't want to take apart another nursery. You may delay sharing the news you're expecting because you hate the prospect of sharing sad news again. For in hope, we were saved. Now hope that is seen is not hope. For who hopes for what is seen? But if we hope for what we do not see, we patiently wait for it. Romans 8:24-25

Pregnancy after loss raises conflicts of anger and jealousy. One strange part of expecting after loss is that you can still envy other pregnant women. Their easy joy, innocent bliss, and assumptions that their baby will simply be born – healthy and alive.

You never get that innocence back, and it's tempting to stew in anger and jealousy. Why did this have to happen to me? Spiritually? The challenge is to seek peace. I don't want to project my story on anyone else's, but I'm not the same person I used to be. So, I try to befriend myself and practice mercy on my heart in the ways I imagine God does, too. Pregnancy after loss knows you cannot control it. Spiritually? The challenge is to practice humility.

Our hope comes from our confidence in God's sovereignty, character, and promises. When we read "all things work together for good," Romans. 8:28, that good isn't necessarily the growth of our family; we read it and are comforted that God works all things for his glory, which is inexplicably tied to our good. We're confident he will use this experience to make us more like Jesus, to teach us to trust him, and to give us the ability to comfort others. But our greatest hope comes from the finished work of Jesus. Those who hope in him lack no good thing. We aren't immune to suffering.

Life can change in an instant. This is our first experience as a couple with true grief. Our married life has been relatively free of trouble apart from the relational consequences of our selfishness and sin. This experience reminds us that being followers of Jesus doesn't mean everything will go well. The Bible is clear that being a Christian means, we can expect to suffer.

We're grateful for the opportunity to be near Jesus by being acquainted with sorrow. May we always be so protected from loving ease and finding security in our circumstances as we've been the past few days. It's not 'all for nothing.'

I'm tempted to resent my lingering pregnancy symptoms and believe this was a cruel joke. "What's the point?" the enemy whispers as he seeks to enter my mind through the doorway of cynicism. But in the kingdom of God, nothing is wasted. He works all things for good. Enduring this nausea and fatigue may not be rewarded with the birth of a baby, but suffering makes me more like Jesus, and I have an inheritance kept for me in heaven that cannot perish. The secret things belong to God.

Let Him have all your worries and cares, for He is always thinking about you and watching everything that concerns you. I Peter 5:7, TLB
Miscarriages No More!

I AM AN OVERCOMER, I SURVIVED!

Acknowledgments

I want to first and foremost acknowledge Abba Father for being such a Great Father, Jesus my Savior, Redeemer, Restorer, And Life Giver, The Person of the Holy Spirit being my Teacher and Friend. I am extremely grateful to my mother, LeDoris Allen, for her love, prayer, caring, and sacrifices. I am very thankful to my wife, Yvette Callahan, and our children for their love, understanding, and continued support, Apostle Paul Easley and Apostle Daniel LeBlanc, for holding me Accountable to the Truth of the Word and the Charter of Jesus Christ. To Dr. Elaine Harvey for the Opportunity to be part of such a Movement of God and all the Great work flowing through Her Assignment from Abba Father. To All my Brothers and Sisters in the Realm of the Spirit and Household of Faith, Blessings, Honor, and Much Love and Grace!

Soaring International Ministries
Contact me on Facebook @ Ricky James Allen-Callahan
Phone 225 573 3339

But those who wait for the Lord [who expect, look for, and hope in Him] Will gain new strength and renew their power; They will lift up their wings [and rise up close to God] like eagles [rising toward the sun]; They will run and not become weary, They will walk and not grow tired. Isaiah 40:31 AMP

A Great Work: Finishing Strong with No More
Spiritual Miscarriage
Fresh From the Press

I AM AN OVERCOMER, I SURVIVED!

About Ricky James Allen-Callahan

Soaring High As The Eagle Father Set My Heart and Mind on You.

Give Me Your Vision For My Future. Help me to see myself the way you see me. So that I can Imagine and live in The Blessing, You have in store for me.

(The Voice of a 12-Year-Old.)

RICKY JAMES ALLEN-CALLAHAN

But those who wait for the Lord [who expect, look for, and hope in Him] shall change and renew their strength and power; they shall lift their wings and mount up [close to God] as eagles [mount up to the sun]; they shall run and not be weary, they shall walk and not faint or become tired. [Heb.12:1-3.] Isaiah 40:31 AMPC

Ricky James Allen-Callahan was born on August 25, 1969, to the Parents, Ledoris Allen and Harrison Morris Callahan, Jr. Ricky is a 1987 Graduate of Zachary High School and a Graduate of ITI Technical College Baton Rouge, La.

Ricky attained his First Job at The Lodge Restaurant until it was destroyed by fire. At 17, Ricky received his Driver's License and purchased his first automobile with the money earned on his first job. Ricky was a local driver truck for Flowers Bakery Company. Dows Chemical Plant. He is a retired employee of Shell Chemical Plant.

Ricky is the Blessed Husband of Yvette L. Callahan. Proud Father of Christian(Cartana), Dana (Rufus Sr.), Chaz(Tariel), and Carnell, Proud Grandfather of Cerenity, Jace, Rufus Jr, Makynzi, Madisyn.

Ricky was Baptized in October 1992 by The Late Pastor Sam Marshal Johnson at the St. Peter B. Church. Ricky taught Sunday School and Bible Study at St. Peter

I AM AN OVERCOMER, I SURVIVED!

B. Church. After moving to Baton Rouge, Louisiana, Ricky became a member of Living Faith Christian Center Pastor Raymond Johnson.

Minister Ricky Callahan is defined by his peers as a Gentle Giant humble yet Powerful Intercessor, prolific, prophetic, and Apostolic voice for the Nation. Student of the Word.

Ricky encounters the Revelation of Heaven and Hell as an infant and begins operating as a seer at the age of 12. Through several Angelic Visitations. God made a demand on his life through visitation. God gave him His Vision of "Soaring International Ministries," A FIVEFOLD FULL GOSPEL GLOBAL MINISTRY (Acts 5:20, Ephesians 4:11-13). Minister Ricky Callahan walks in the supernatural, Operating in the Glory Realm, sensitive to the Person of the Holy Spirit's encounter with God. Minister Ricky Callahan has been given the ability to make the supernatural practical to people who believe there is something more. Minister Ricky Callahan has a Doctor of Leadership Theology Degree from Bethany World Prayer Center and 13 weeks of Discipleship (Encountering God) from Doers of the Word Ministry. He was knowing & Doing the Will of God, a Life history of teaching from the Holy Spirit.

Co-laboring in a unified and balanced pursuit of the Great Commission of Our Lord, Jesus Christ. We are commissioned to steward a multi-ethnic, multi-cultural

21st Century Church to raise a hedge of protection over our homes, cities, nation, and world while effectively ministering to people of diverse social, economic, and ethnic backgrounds. We are called to unite them in Kingdom Love and Purpose by preaching the Gospel of the Kingdom and teaching the "uncompromising" Word of God.

Perspective Words from Evangelist Colton Butler:
Mighty Man of God, Prayer Warrior. Wisdom of God. Overflowing with the God kind of Faith and the Love of God and Life & Light, joy, peace, patience, kindness, goodness, gentleness, faithfulness, and self-control. Fun & Funny. Happy. Enjoys life. Selfless. Listener. Peacemaker. Righteous. Obedient. Good & Faithful Servant. Effective communicator. Fervent. Powerful. Strong. Bold. Courageous. Blessed & Highly Favored. Blessed to be a blessing. Generous. Steadfast. Immovable. Always Abounding in the Work of the Lord. Fruitful. In tune with the heart of God & the Holy Spirit in Jesus' name Amen Glory to God.

I AM AN OVERCOMER, I SURVIVED!

Cancer Did Not Win…By LaKeisha J. Richards

I didn't die. I lived! And now I'm telling the world what God did. God tested me, he pushed me hard, but he didn't hand me over to Death. Swing wide the city gates—the righteous gates! I'll walk right through and thank God! This Temple Gate belongs to God, so the victors can enter and praise." (Psalms 118:17-20 MSG)

As a teenager, I used to suffer from heavy menstrual cycles and painful cramps. As a young woman, I dreaded that time of the month. I was under the impression that the older I became, the easier my menstrual cycles would be. Boy, was that far from the truth. It was the complete opposite. The bleeding became more and more intense, and the cramps were unbearable. I remember during the summer months of 2010, I could tell that something wasn't quite right, and some changes were going on in my body then. I felt that it was important that I reach out to my primary care provider to advise him of my concerns. During this visit, the Dr. wanted me to take birth control pills to see if that would help slow down the bleeding. Birth control was never my thing, nor would this be the solution to the problem. Finally, my Dr. thought it would be a good idea for me to see a Gynecologist. During my visit, he expressed a few concerns, and after running a few tests, I received news from my Gynecologist that I had a growing cyst and needed surgery. After having surgery to remove the cyst, my then Dr felt the need to do some further testing.

    I remember it as if it was yesterday. Suddenly out of nowhere, the unknown was about to become my reality. Life was about to be accurate, and I never imagined the adjustments that would soon take place. My life was turned upside down on this beautiful sunny day in June of 2010. My doctor then diagnosed me with a rare ovarian cancer type. Do you talk about life happening? I became devastated and confused. This was something that I had never imagined hearing. No one wants to hear the C word, but there I was, and it hit me like a ton of bricks. My Dr looked at me and said, "Ms. Richards, I'm so sorry to have to tell you this, but the cyst has come back malignant."

    At that point, I was dumbfounded because I didn't know what that meant. However, I could tell it wasn't good by the look on his face. In other words, it's cancerous, and he didn't know how to treat it; therefore, he needed to refer me to a cancer specialist at Duke University. As I looked at the Dr., I completely shut everything coming out of his mouth. There I was in the office all alone with no words. I didn't know whether to break down and cry or scream at the top of my lungs. Once reality sat in, I heard him telling me that he felt confident I would be okay because it was in the early stages. You must understand that when most women are diagnosed with ovarian cancer, it's in the final stage. It's a silent killer, and there is currently no cure. Oh, but I know a man name JESUS! He's my Healer, and God is greater than any cancer or obstacle you may face. Once my doctor's visit was over, I remember sitting in the car for 20-30 minutes trying to figure out how or when I would share the news with my family.

With tears streaming down my face, I pray and petition God for healing while reminding him of HIS WORD! In that conversation, I told the Lord I was too young to die and that my children would not grow up without their mothers. After sitting in the car, I decided to go to the mall and window shop. After all, I still had a 45-minute drive home. I decided to call my mother (who is also my Apostle) to inform her of my diagnosis. Her soothing, calm, encouraging voice spoke to my spirit and declared "Divine Healing" over her baby girl. She prayed over me and assured me that everything would be just fine. I can't even imagine the emotions or the thoughts that were going through her mind during those moments of that conversation over the phone.

Later that evening, when I arrived home, I called a family meeting to share the news with my immediate family (my children, brother, and our Assistant Pastor). No one was expecting to hear what I would say next. Trying to stay strong for my children, I knew I had to fight no matter what, and I was determined to WIN! I heard the Holy Spirit say that this sickness would not be unto death in those moments. No, it is for God's glory so that God's Son may be glorified through it (John 11:4). Even though I wasn't quite sure all that God had for me to do, I knew that I couldn't die without fulfilling my purpose here on the earth. I knew someone somewhere needed to hear my testimony and find hope that if I made it, they too could and would make it as well. I don't know, but that someone could very well be YOU! At that moment, I was reminded that it was no longer about me.

Long story short, after proceeding with my last surgery, God proved himself to be faithful as only he could! That was in June 2010; this year, I celebrated 12 years of being "Cancer Free"! What a MIGHTY GOD we serve! Millions didn't make it, but I'm one who did, and it's only by the Grace of God. Today, I can assure you that in the midst of it all, He turned my mourning into dancing and my pain into purpose.

I AM AN OVERCOMER, I SURVIVED!

As long as there's life, there is hope. Your obstacle may not be cancer; it could be diabetes, multiple sclerosis, HIV/Aids, Lupus, a wayward child, a financial dilemma, or an unfaithful spouse—Trust me when I say God wants to heal those areas in your life that hurts the most. That includes mind, body, and soul—Healing is available to you...receive it in Jesus' Name!

No matter who you are or the obstacles you may face in your life. All that matters is that you are still here, making you a survivor. I want to pause and prophetically decree the Word of the Lord over your life. Come in agreement with me as I prophesy that YOU shall not die, but LIVE and declare (proclaim) the works of the Lord (Psalms 118:17). I don't care how difficult it may be. It's important what you believe. It's even more important what you speak out of your mouth. Life and death are in the power of your tongue (Proverbs 18:21). I command you to SPEAK LIFE and LIVE! Speak it when you feel like it, and speak it when you don't!

On this journey called life, we are presented with tests and trials, such as sickness, betrayals, finances, divorce, and so on. Not to mention that we are now more than ever living in times where the faith of every human being on the face of this earth is being tested as never before.

No matter what you face in life, God has many ways he communicates with us to confirm his promises. His word will spring up at the right time to remind us of His power and grace. "For my thoughts are not your thoughts, neither are your ways my ways, declares the Lord. As the heavens are higher than the earth, so are my ways higher than your ways and my thoughts than your thoughts." -Isaiah 55:8-9 KJV

Because He knew me before I was formed in my mother's womb, it's not my job to understand the how's or whys, but I trust God. I'll be the first to admit that that can be easier said than done at times. Trusting God is never easy; however, it is a requirement.

As believers, we are to trust God. We must trust in knowing that He has a plan for us. He's a good father who knows what we need before asking. "It shall come to pass that before they call, I will answer; And while they are still speaking, I will hear." -Isaiah 65:24 KJV.

Guess what? I don't know what God's plan is for your life. I don't know every detail he has for my life either. His word reminds us that He is the author and perfecter of our faith. He created us in his image and knows each day and year of our lives, and nothing we will ever say, do or experience in life will ever catch him by surprise because he knows us one by one and name by name.

Your eyes saw my unformed body; all the days ordained for me were written in your book before one of them came to be." – Psalm 139:16

What do you do when you have dreams and set goals for your life that you want to fulfill? These dreams and goals bring excitement into your life, and you start the work toward making your dreams a reality. Then you run into roadblocks, or the unexpected happens. You pause and deal with it, but you never give up! What do you do when LIFE Happens?

In my conclusion, my friend, let me encourage you that there will be obstacles along the way. However, I want to share some good news you can overcome them all! Obstacles don't mean failure. It simply means you are growing and becoming a better version of YOU. I am an OVERCOMER! For this reason, I can boldly proclaim, To God Be The Glory, Cancer did not win...

LAKEISHA J. RICHARDS

Acknowledgments

I thank God for every opportunity he blesses me to share my testimony with others. Dr. Pastor Elaine Harvey, thank you for being sensitive to the Holy Spirit in birthing this amazing anthology. I'm grateful to be a part of your vision. Special thanks to my family and friends, who are always in my corner to support me. I love you all!

I AM AN OVERCOMER, I SURVIVED!

Prophetess LaKeisha J. Richards

Mildly put, LaKeisha J. Richards is a powerhouse! Her titles are many. Amongst them are bestselling Author, Prophetess, Ordained Minister, CEO, Certified Life Coach, Christian

Chaplain, and Ambassador of the highly acclaimed platform "Don't Give up on Love 2.0."

LaKeisha is a professional speaker and coach on the John Maxwell team. She has also appeared on Dominion TV and The Fierce, Ignition & Activation Radio Show. She has been featured in KISH Magazine (nominated on the Top 25 Global Influencer list and Top 24 Women Who Win list), Kishma George Radio Show, and the Nicole LIVE Radio Show, just to name a few. She is also the TV Host of The LaKeisha J. Richards Show featured on The Zenith TV Network.

LaKeisha resides in North Carolina. With her mission clear, she continues to serve faithfully in ministry. Her platform, "Don't Give Up on Love 2.0," is available on all her social media sites. She also has several books that can be purchased. To contact for speaking engagements, contact her at: www.ljrichards.com or on her various social media platforms.

Facebook: LaKeisha J. Richards
Instagram: MsLaKeishaJRichards
Clubhouse: LaKeisha J. Richards

Surviving Divorce: Broken Vows Behind The Veil
By Cheryl Richard

After being married for 22 years, I never thought the day would come when marriage would end for me. Having three children, two of whom were in college, but I will tell anyone that when you have Christ in your life, he can help you through any impossible situation. And we must have people on our side that we can trust. We must have a heart of forgiveness because you can make it through anything it may seem impossible. You may have those moments where it looks like you can't even make it through the next day; furthermore, it seems like you can't even make it to the next moment. Because when I was going through the divorce, I ended up losing my home losing my job because of the mental stress and financial crisis I had to file for bankruptcy. But in all of that, God still made provision. I couldn't give up. He was there for me. I had to have a prayer life. I had to have a life of depending totally upon God. Talking to people I know would give me what I needed to hear, not what I wanted to hear—blocking out all the naysayers, trusting in God with all my heart, and leading not to my understanding.

I tried to filter what was going on; it would only bring confusion, so with the hardship coming on and becoming homeless after going to the divorce, it was due to infidelity. I was able to have shelter when someone opened their home for me after being homeless. I survived being homeless now. I now have a place to give back and help homeless people. I went from living off two thousand dollars a week to six dollars a week; I still made it. I still survived, so it's not about what you have but what you do with what you have. The word of God tells us that if we are faithful over a few, He'll make us rulers over many. At the time in my life when I felt like there was no hope at all, I felt suicidal, and when that happened, I knew then I had to reach beyond a break and hold on. And you, too, can hold on. Nothing is impossible for you to get through. We got to be that nail on the wall for each other. Hold on when you want to fall and throw in the towel. If you can't do anything else, you think of pure things, thinking of good and not of evil.

We must have a heart of forgiveness and an agape love walk. Find the good in every situation. It may be that, yes, pain is going to come through life pressure is going to come, but we must press through it. We got to go through the process when we take a journey. When we're on our way to a place, there may be detours as we go down a natural highway. I always say that the spirit and nature run parallel. Every part of the body serves a purpose. The eyes can't do what the feet do, and vice versa. There's a purpose for everything that we go through. We got to pull ourselves through, and we can only go through it through faith.

His perfect time and He has a perfect plan for us. We must pray, trust and wait, not rush. Delayed isn't a denial. Just believe in His word and be fully persuaded. What He has promised, he is also able to perform. I survived. My kids weren't able to go to finish college because of the mental distress from what their parents had gone through. They didn't give up and stood strong. They held on to hope in this situation. Sometimes my children will tell me things like they're happy. So, we have to be careful in presenting ourselves to others because we never know who is watching us. We can't lose the witness. We have to lead by example. We have to be a light to shine before men so they can see our good works.

I don't care what nobody else is doing. You have to walk in your authority and stand in integrity. Know your identity, and don't allow anyone to dictate who you are. You are more than a conqueror. You are the apple of God's eye. So, no matter what you go through, know that you can survive. No matter the obstacles, trials, and tribulations that come your way, you will survive. There was a point in my life when I didn't even have a vehicle, but I still made it. Stand on faith and His word. We can't let what we see determine our outcome. Faith is the substance of things hoped for and the evidence of things not seen. So, what we have, He has granted us. You can speak an encouraging word to others and pray for others. The enemy can't do any more than what God allows him to do. God gets all the glory.

We will stand on what we believe and His promises. We believe in his word because it never returns back void. You call those things into existence, command, and decree it. You can put the blood of Jesus on it! You have the power on the inside of you. Greater is He that is in me than in the world. You can speak life or death out of your mouth. One of my favorite commercials is the power of 1 voice. What are you saying? Speak positively. Be careful of what you allow to enter your temple. Keep yourself anointed as a temple of the Holy Ghost. Your body belongs to God. So, we must take care of it just as we take care of our tangible things.

Someone needs to hear your testimony because you survived. I'll be able to stand and tell someone else that nobody but God did this. You, too, can get through it! Yes, the days will come when it seems like you can't get through it. The tears may fall, but allow those tears to be water to plant your future. In the beginning, was the word. The word was with God, and the word was God. He spoke everything into existence, so you have a right to speak those things into existence. If you need a home, He can give you a home. If you need a car and finances, he can give you whatever your need. He is our provider. He will never leave us nor forsake us. When I felt weak, he was strong in me. He had others praying me through. God has granted you with gifts. Therefore, don't allow the storms of life to take your desires, passion, and zeal away. No storm lasts forever. Weeping may endure for a night, but joy comes in the morning. What God has blessed, no man can curse. Ask God to create a clean heart and renew the right spirit within you.

    Have a heart of forgiveness even towards the person who mistreated you. For two years, I said empty, but all I was doing was holding myself back. I was holding my blessings back. God can get you through if you just hold on and keep the faith. There is nothing too hard for God to do. Always remember that God will never fail. His word always fights for you. The race is not given to the swift nor the strong but to those who hold out and endure to the end. I'm grateful to be a vessel to empower others and speak life. After the Vows were Broken Behind the Veil. I became a Voice of Virtue to give H.O.P.E. Helping Other People Emerge, never forgetting who and how I survived. Giving praise, honor, and glory for all I have been through and attesting HIS WORD is True. Having Favor to go where needed and connections with the right people to help lead. Knowing that HE would enlarge my territory and HIS hand is with me, and it would keep me from evil, and it wouldn't cause pain because, at the end of it all, I SURVIVED. I GAINED.

I, Cheryl Denise Richard, Dedicate this Chapter of my Life to my Beloved Deceased Father "Bennie Richard, Sr) Love- Your Queen

Acknowledgments

I give all the glory, honor, and praise to my Lord and Savior, Jesus Christ. I am eternally grateful to my family, Ruby Richard (mother), Children, Ronald Dixon, Jr. (Brittany), Ishmeil Lee (Delveckio), and ZaVaun Dixon, Sr. (Tenisha.) I am thankful for my Grandchildren, among other family members. Thank you to my Intercessory Prayer Partners and friends.

I am also most glorified for "all those" whom I have had the pleasure to work with and connect to during my transitioning while going through the process and current assignments well: Angela Green, Simone Higgin Botham, Curtis Day, Lachaela Wells, Theresa Perkins, Coach Regina Mullen, Shadow Worldz Radio, WPFC-Pastor Ralph Moore, Elder Cassandra Lang, Erica Smart, Prophet Frank Delaney, Pamela Johnson, Chermelita Lafayete, and Pastor Elaine Harvey (allowing me the opportunity to write this chapter.

Voices of Virtue Sponsors and Partners. Atlanta Brand Agency- Production Company for the Reality TV Show along with the Cast/Crew of "SURVIVING DIVORCE" (Reality TV w/ a Twist).

Special Thanks to Mitchell Pitts, Martha Williams, Katherine Lavine, Tracy Hawkins, Patrice Johnson, Sonja Green, Erica Trams, and HPC. Eternal

Thanks to Everyone, even Names not listed yet, in Heart and Spirit forever Love. To all who have provided me with extensive Spiritual, personal, and Professional guidance and helped me in my walk of Faith during my season of Brokenness to Breakthroughs. I Survived. I'm an Overcomer!

Romans 4:21 "I am fully persuaded what God has promised He is also able to perform."

HOW TO CONTACT THE AUTHOR:

NAME: Cheryl Denise "Dee' Richard

EMAILS: voicesofvirtue22@gmail.com

vovpower@gmail.com

royalfashionsandessentials@gmail.com

WEBSITES: www.voicesofvirtue.org

www.royalfashionsandessentials.com

Social Media Sites:

https://www.facebook.com/voicesofvirtue22

https://www.podserve.fm/w/voicesofvirtue

https://youtube.com/channel/UCKzfo1uvRnxQs8mWlj OUJJQ

PHONE: 225.577.3436 OR 225.241.8132

I AM AN OVERCOMER, I SURVIVED!

About - Cheryl D. Richard

C.E.O/Founder/President/Executive Producer

Greetings! I would like to graciously introduce myself. My name is Cheryl D. Richard. Although, I am fondly known as "Dee" to my fellow Batchelor, LA native. I am a proud mother of three children (Ronald Jr., Ishmeil, and ZaVaun. Also, I have ten grandchildren. My

mother, Ruby Weir-Richard is one of my greatest cheerleaders.

I serve with agape' of love in my heart, and hands. I adore people, we are all made in God's image; therefore, it is easy for me to love, give, and forgive. In this life, I have learned to not take no person for granted. God plants others in our lives for various reasons. I do not regret my interaction with anyone, who has partaken in my life. Many individuals have passed through my life. The Lord has removed people from my life; actually, some of those individuals had caused pain in my life. Each person was placed in my life to help me get in position for my divine destiny and purpose.

I quit worrying about the how(s) in my life; because I know who Jesus was. If I would have chosen to worry, I would have not needed to pray. If I exercised my right to pray, I did not need to worry. I believe in Word and Worship in life; it works! An honest attempt would immensely beat failure! I have learned to cease making excuses, in order to pursue my purpose. An excuse is merely a lie on a crutch! I had to stay focused! I had to go through the process to reach progression! I am a blood bought believer in Deuteronomy 28:1-14. I am fully persuaded that God can perform what he has promised. If I commit my works to the Lord, my plans shall be established.

As I've traveled through this journey of life; I have faced many detours. However, I have learned that I must follow, and use the best G.P.S. (God's Path in Scripture). Things might become delayed; nevertheless, they will not be denied. Most people have visions and dreams concerning their lives. I am no exception! Albeit things do not always go our way. Now, I know that it's okay. It should not go my way; things should go God's way! I ended up getting pregnant on prom night, and I got married at the age of twenty. Nevertheless, God gave me three seeds in which those three lives gave me joy to live every second. Sometimes, poor decisions are birthed through bad experiences. I've been around the mountains, and through the valleys. My season of homelessness catapulted my desire to help the Homeless; provide shelter and essentials (Virtue of H.O.P.E.) Helping Other People Emerge. An outreach has manifested "Voices of Virtue", evincing love and hope. I authored a poem called "A Lover Like Jesus Is All I Need." I'm also the visionary of a Reality TV Show "Surviving Divorce" to empower and evince others.

I am on an Outreach Mission as a vessel with a voice being a servitor with an outpouring of Voices of Virtue. VOV has established and rendered services for the community, individual bases, and other masses. In which some includes:

CHERYL RICHARD

*Speaker *Poet *Confidante *Talk Show/Podcast Host *Online Apparel Store

www.voicesofvirtue.org

www.royalfashionsandessentials.com

I AM AN OVERCOMER, I SURVIVED!

Life's Afflictions
By Cassandra Lang

My life started off being rejected. My mother tried to abort me. She took quinine to get rid of me, but it didn't work. She had just had my sister and lied to welfare, saying she didn't know who the father was because she didn't want to put my dad on child support. She told me she was swiping one day, and the Lord told her, "If you abort this child, you will be dead this time next week." After all, they were cohabiting.

On this journey, I experienced much pain. At the age of five, I was molested by my step-grandfather, which happened to be a preacher. That truly affected me as an adult. I wasn't promiscuous, but this encounter hovered a spirit of lust over me. Older men would always gravitate to me. They would proposition me. I believe the enemy played on my desire to have a father figure in my life. But later learned that a man cannot give you the love of your father. I can remember going to see my father in the nursing home. He hugged me and told me he loved me. That was the hug I had been searching for. Despite him not being present in my life, that was the purest hug I have ever had. I wrapped and cried in his arms.

I got married at the age of 22; I can remember crying during sexual intercourse. Because I felt that men just wanted my body and not me. I've always felt rejected. We moved from California to Louisiana when I was 12 years old. We stayed for a summer. My mom went back to California to work, save money and relocate. Meanwhile, we were being cared for by my grandmother. I can remember my uncle trying to molest my sister. I was so afraid, so I told my great aunt. She shared it with my grandmother. Later that day, my grandmother took me to the backyard and beat me for telling it. From there, I experienced more pain. One of the leaders that I trusted advanced me. He had me thinking it was okay to fornicate. I was in my middle 20's. After my divorce, I knew it was wrong, but he was older, and she was a leader. He convinced me that it was okay. I didn't know the word. I was a baby in Christ.

He would say, "David in the Bible committed adultery, and he was the apple of God's eye."

So, this went on for seven years. There were times I'd cry before intercourse with him. My spirit was so grieved. What tore me apart was when he married another woman—bitterness on top of bitterness. The church hurt was another layer of pain. By now, because of the pains of life, I'm angry and hate people. I'd created a wall, a brick wall. I was doing ministry and bleeding emotionally. See, the devil's job is to catch you when you're young, defile you, and take you out literally. But Glory is to God; He blocked it.

But I will say that it was good that I was afflicted. While I was on my bed of affliction, I had time to reflect. God had time to perform emotional surgery. To free me from the prison I was in. He tore down the strongholds of my mind. When I tell you he healed me from the pain. I forgave those who hurt me. I am free. Free indeed. There's nothing too hard for God to do. He can heal your soul. He touched my soul with His finger of love.

The very thing the enemy tried to use to take me out. God is using it to bless people. So know that your pain has not been in vain. Healing from the pain creates oil, the anointing. Let me share a story about the oil. In 2 Kings 4, it talks about the Widow woman. Her husband died, and she had a debt to pay. The creditors were after her sons to make them slaves. The prophet knocked on her door; he proceeded with a question. He asked her, "What's in your house of value?"

She responded by saying, "nothing but a saved pot of oil."

The prophet began to give her instructions. He said, "Go to town and borrow some vessels, not a few.

Bring those vessels back and pour your oil into the vessels. Go back to town, sell those vessels, pay your debt, and live off the rest."

I shared this story to encourage you to package your story and use it to pour into people. To change their life, the very thing the enemy used to take you out, God's going to use to set others FREE...after you have suffered, God will establish you and settle you. All things work together for the good of those who love the Lord and have been called for His purpose. It's time for you to pour out your oil.

Here's my recent testimony. I'll say it was good I was afflicted. It healed my soul.

Three Years After My Affliction

The Lord spoke to me and said, "Live with It."

This is not eternal; it is temporal. While in the nursing home, the Holy Spirit gave me a book titled "Mind Confessions," which I am publishing. The revelation the Holy Spirit gave me during that time has been lifesaving. My scripture was I shall live and not die. After almost dying, overcoming; septic, having a toe amputated, having a dramatic heart attack, and having to get on dialysis, on top of that, living in a Nursing home. My Nephrologist told me which at that time, I was 280 lbs., and 100 of it was fluid in my body. I could barely move. She told me, "Right now, your body is in the condition of an 80-year-old woman. You are going to have to be patient with yourself."

I held on to that. She encouraged me. She told me everything was going to be fine in time. Depression fell on me. I refused Physical therapy for nine months. I stayed in bed. One Thanksgiving, my brother came to get me from the nursing home to spend Thanksgiving with him and his family. To my surprise, I could not stand it. I had lost muscle (muscle atrophy). So now, another challenge, learning to walk again. It took me two years to regain my strength to stand, but through months of therapy, I gained enough strength to stand and take steps with a walker. Only to break a leg while walking with the Physical Therapist during therapy. That setback plundered me into depression due to my belief in God for a kidney transplant. I was waiting to get on the transplant list. One of the requirements was that I would have to be able to walk. However, I was determined to walk again.

To update you, I am walking again with the assistance of a roll-aid walker. My goal is to walk without the walker. I shared my testimony to encourage you to" live with it." You shall live and not die and declare the works of the Lord. I've also learned that God will not take until He's ready. That said, you and I are here for GOD'S PURPOSE.

Jeremiah 29:11 For I know the plans I have for you declares the Lord, thoughts of peace, a future a hope an EXPECTED END! Remember, the book of Revelations says, "They were overcome by the blood of the Lamb and the word of their testimony." Share your TESTIMONY!

Acknowledgements

I'd first like to thank God for saving me. I'd also like to thank Pastor Ralph Moore for teaching me the word of God. And for giving me a chance in radio. He trained me basically through me in the water. But it made me; I would say, an awesome radio announcer. I'd also like to thank Bishop Rodney Walker of Waldorf, Maryland, for ordaining me as an Elder and or believing in the gift. My spiritual mother, Pastor Connie Rucker, who poured into me. Pastor Rita Lee. Pastor Evelyn Thomas. My Aunts Carolyn Robins Cynthia Taylor, and my siblings Jewel Taylor, Robin Taylor, and Rudolph Grigsby III, my dear friend Janelle Scott for being my support throughout the years, Korey Miller for encouraging me to write music, and last but not least, Dr. Elaine Harvey, for the opportunity to share my Testimony.

CASSANDRA LANG

About - Cassandra Lang

Cassandra Lang is a graduate of Remington College with a degree in Business Administration. She attended Southern University, with a Scholarship in music. Graduated from, Hope Bible Institute with a Bachelor's Degree in Theology. Former Marketing Director for Gospel Truth

I AM AN OVERCOMER, I SURVIVED!

Magazine (Kerry Douglas), Sales Director for Clear Channel Radio Station. Marketing Director & Account Executive, for WPFC 1550AM. She's a 20-year veteran in Radio. She's the producer & host of the Cassandra Lang Show and Community Empowerment. She has authored Create Your World workbook, I Am a Queen, and Discovering My Self. With a forthcoming book titled Mind Confessions. She's a producer and writer of" Bring Back Your Glory" Live recording. Producer of Meditative Scriptures, Love Thoughts, and Healing Scriptures. She's a Motivator, Encourager, Trainer, Teacher, and an Ordained Elder under the Leadership of Bishop Rodney Walker of God Is in Control Church of Waldorf, Maryland. Lastly, she's the founder of Create Your World Ministries, founded by her in 1996. And she's the founder of Create Your World Wisdom Network Internet Radio Station. Her famous quote is there is only one mind print like yours, only one fingerprint like yours, only one contribution of you, so be sure you contribute.

Check her out on:
Tik Tok
Facebook
YouTube Channel
Instagram
Email: createyourworld2021@gmail.com

Go On, Girl. You are a Queen!
By Felicia McKoy-Laguerre

I am an Overcomer. I Survived!

Can't you see how I drive?
I stop at a red light, looking left and right.
I proceed with caution even without a yellow light
I still hit a bump in the road. Then it begins to rain.
Turn on my windshield wipers. Swish swish swish.
I continue, until an accident happens, and I can't move.
Stopped in my tracks on this journey called life. Where do I begin?
Define overcoming.
Define survival.
A rainbow overcomes the rain.
Everyday Challenges.
I am persevering on a daily basis.
Talk about levels of trauma.
What haven't I experienced?
Your imagination can create images of what may have come next, but the question is, how do you overcome, and how have you survived?
By Felicia McKoy-Laguerre

PTSD. The first time you experience trauma, it leaves you on alert. We can heal from it, but you can't forget it unless it becomes too much that your memory causes you to forget to help you learn how to survive. Anxiety, depression, drug addiction, overlooked, mistreated, cursed out, left behind, and so much more could be your story. If that is not your story, that's ok. Keep living.

What happens to a dream deferred?
Does it dry up
like a raisin in the sun?
Or fester like a sore—
And then run?
Does it stink like rotten meat?
Or crust and sugar over—
like a syrupy sweet?

Maybe it just sags
like a heavy load.
Or does it explode?
Harlem by Langston Hughes

Or you can see yourself like Maya and be just like air and rise. You have to see it before you see it!

I AM AN OVERCOMER, I SURVIVED!

Still I Rise

You may write me down in history
With your bitter, twisted lies,
You may trod me in the very dirt
But still, like dust, I'll rise.

....

Out of the huts of history's shame
I rise
Up from a past that's rooted in pain
I rise
I'm a black ocean, leaping and wide,
Welling and swelling I bear in the tide.

Leaving behind nights of terror and fear
I rise
Into a daybreak that's wondrously clear
I rise
Bringing the gifts that my ancestors gave,
I am the dream and the hope of the slave.
I rise
I rise
I rise.

BY MAYA ANGELOU

Maybe that's not your story. Maybe your story is similar to Esther, how several people overcame and survived. What does it mean to overcome? To overcome most means to get over something. Some people may have to get to a fork in the road. Others may have had to get through a day's work. Others may have to find joy in the morning in any given situation. Ester and Job overcame. To survive meant they lived to tell the story or made it to another day. Let's take a deeper look. Ester was destined to be Queen for a higher purpose. The reality was that it did not happen just that simply. As we read in the book of Esther, Esther had to hide her identity to become Queen Esther. Have you ever had to hide who you were to survive your circumstances?

Yes, we probably never really looked at this text like such. She had to wear a mask from her husband. To become queen, she had to undergo an entire year of cleansing. She had to mask for an entire year to spare her life and an entire community of lives. Understand that cleansing and masking do not go hand in, in hand in the spiritual sense. Even in her new marriage, she had to carry the burden of a secret. So even after she became Queen, she had to carry this secret. Any married woman understands that pillow talk with her husband is a hard place to mask and keep secrets. There is where true intimacy is supposed to happen. Esther had to wait until the appointed time to unmask, overcome, and survive her situation. Imagine how hard, gruesome, and withdrawn or coy she had to be with her husband up until that point. I could feel her pain. Stomach in knots, fear mounting up, lump in your throat, sweating profusely, heart in your throat. And the pressure that makes you withdrawn and not able to enjoy the full honeymoon of being a new wife. Think about the pressure and fear of being cast out and killed, all the planning and praying she had to do too. However, we know that Esther overcame and survived. She overcame the loss of her parents and the burden of being a Jew. She overcame the guilt of holding a grave secret from her husband.

Often in our situations, we focus on our pain. We often tend to focus on the pain and not that she survived. Look at Job, a man who lost his children, wife, friends, and worldly possessions. He not only overcame all of this, but HE also Survived.

I, to have a similar testimony of survival. Most people look at me and think I am just a sweet, beautiful face. They often don't understand that I have overcome and survived many things. Come with me to look at my life.

At birth, my mom left and left me behind for my grandmother to raise me. So, from the beginning, I was abandoned. If you know, as I know, when you are abandoned, especially at birth, it leaves you vulnerable. Psychologists today also state that spanked children are often traumatized and never the same. Well, I was spanked with switches, extension cords, belts, shoes, brooms, and whatever my grandmother could get her hands on. I have been abused in many ways, mistreated, talked about, overlooked, left out, and whatever else you can imagine. Can't just you sense the pain?

However, I'm here today to tell you I overcame and survived. My parents were drug addicts, but God allowed me to survive addiction. My mother was once a prostitute, a drug addict, and diagnosed bipolar, but God allowed me to survive. My father, whom I never knew personally, was a veteran, came home addicted to heroin and struggled with it most of his life. My parents did jail/prison on several accounts, but I survived that. I grew up in poverty, where my grandfather often said proudly, "Baby, we is poor."

I overcame and survived poverty. I am the first in my family to maintain a career job for over 20 years, to own a home, survive drug addiction in my right mind, and have a college degree. Thanks be to God!

No matter where you currently find yourself, you can overcome and survive. You may be in active drug addiction, prostitution, sexual trauma, homeless, mentally bound, motherless, fatherless, or even jobless, but you, too, can change or leave that situation no matter how dire it feels. How about none of those are your struggles? It doesn't matter what it is; He loves and desires for you to survive and overcome. The word of God says that nothing is impossible with him.

Luke 18:27 says, "What is impossible with man is possible with God."

You may be facing eviction, but God. I am a witness. I was jobless for an entire year in the midst of Covid with barely any income, but I am still in my home. Glory be to God. You may be a single mom or dad struggling to make ends meet, but God. You might be famous like Twitch with a gift of dance but struggling severely in your mind. Your mind can be rocking with anxiety and depression, but is anything too hard for God? Remember, Esther was motherless and fatherless and became queen. Everything was taken from Job, and in the end, he was restored double for his trouble.

Jeremiah 32:17 says, "Lord, you have made heaven and earth by your great power and outstretched arm. Nothing is too hard for our God."

Let me brag about my Father, whose word says, "The Lord himself goes before you and will be with you; he will never leave nor forsake you. Do not be afraid; do not be discouraged." Deuteronomy 31:8.

I am a witness that nothing is too hard for God. Forget what the saints of old said. God loves you. From the palace to the prison of your mind. He wants us to walk by faith and not by sight. It does matter what the reality is; he wants us to speak to those things that are not as they are. He wants to do exceedingly abundantly above all you can think or ask. He is just waiting for you to trust Him and call on Him. You and I could make our bed in hell. The word says the Lord will rescue us, help us, and give us the power to overcome and survive. Psalm 139:8 (paraphrased).

    The Lord is saying this, no matter who you call yourself, someone has called you, or you have been told. You are a King kid and He loves you and me. You and I can survive any obstacle, pitfall, self-sabotage, ignorance, addiction, debt, mental illness, marriage, sexual situation, homeless, no family, trauma, sexual abuse; you name it, the Lord knows about it, and he can deliver you. I've learned that a true deliverer comes through telling your story. While you help another get delivered, you can provoke the hand of God for your deliverance. God is no respecter of persons. He loves us all. The awesome thing about being a child of God is that He already knows his plans for our life. Whatever we need to overcome, he allowed it to show us our need for Him. He allowed it to show you that there is nothing too hard for him if we Believe and trust in Him. I am an overcomer and have survived to tell you that you, too, must stay! Remember, it is not enough to overcome. God wants you to Survive. Queen or King, you must rise, dream again, and rise. Go on, King/Queen, You are a Survivor. The only thing left is for you to believe it!

Acknowledgments

I am writing this chapter in this book to encourage men/women/youth not to give up on Life. If God said it, it is so! Let nothing get in your way of believing; if God calls you to something, He will do it; his Word tells us He will never leave or forsake us. No matter the obstacles, you can do everything through Christ who strengthens you. I am especially thankful to God for never leaving me through my many trials and tribulations and allowing me to overcome much and to tell and share it.

I'm thankful to Rev Dr. Elaine Harvey for her vision and obedience to write this book and open it up to others to be used by God. Thank God for the people who continue to pray for me and encourage me, and especially for my princes (Faahkari and Edouard Jr.). Sons' there is the greatest in you; never forget that you are both King kids. For my students who also encourage Ms. McKoy to keep writing, you all have power and goodness within you all too.

To all of you, I am eternally grateful.

FELICIA MCKOY-LAGUERRE

About - Felicia McKoy-Laguerre

Felicia McKoy-Laguerre is the CEO/ Author/ Trainer/ Coach/ Doula/ Herbalist/ Speaker/ and Consultant of The Real McKoy Services LLC, where she coaches, writes/prepares customized training, facilitates workshops, prepares mentors, speaks on various platforms, prepares contracts for various businesses, and so much more. She has worked for several organizations teaching and training for over 20 years. She is passionate about mentoring and building the self-esteem of youth and women. She customizes/makes herbs for all your wellness needs. She is a life coach in all aspects of life, from birth, weight loss, career development, family planning, life planning, and beyond.

She has a Bachelor of Arts in Human Services with a concentration in Urban Planning and Community Development. Before graduating, she worked as a Program Supervisor/Trainer for Baltimore Healthy Start/Healthy Families America since 2002, where she worked with women and children. She is currently pursuing her Master's in Education/Counseling and working to become a licensed doula. She truly believes her business is about a person's body, soul, and spirit. She is a co-author of the book Her World; Wisdom & Inspiration From Women In Business, Use What's In Your Hand, and The Greatest Story Never Told. She also has another business: Custom Creations Bling with Paparazzi. Felicia is the mother of two adorable princes: Faahkari and Edouard Jr.

Contact Information:
Felicia McKoy-Laguerre
443-304-7070
teerealmckoy@gmail.com
https://biy.ly/3uXHCuu
www.paparazziaccessories.com/customcreationsbling

FELICIA MCKOY-LAGUERRE

FB: Felicia McKoy-Laguerre or The Real McKoy Coaching, Doula, Herbs, and Training Services, LLC

Instagram: Custom Creations Bling and The Real McKoy Services

I AM AN OVERCOMER, I SURVIVED!

Live and Not Die
By Dr. Juliet Pinder-McBride

On July 5, 2015, a Monday morning, I felt a hand shake my left shoulder. I looked to see if someone was waking me up, but to my surprise, no one was there. I looked at the clock on the wall. It was 9:00 am. I was in another state away from my home in New York City. I spoke at two churches in Goldsboro, North Carolina, the day before. I was staying at my niece's house. She ran into the room, tried to pick me up, and when I looked at her, she said, "Auntie, why is your face twisted?"

As I began to get up to go to the bathroom, this is before I fell to the floor three times. Unfortunately, this is when I realized something was wrong with me.

During all the commotion, I heard the spirit of God tell me with such calm and power, "What you are going through is only temporary because I'm going to heal you. Take pictures to document as evidence." I looked at my nephew and moved my right finger to motion to take pictures; he understood the assignment. By this time, the EMS had rushed me to

Wayne County Hospital. Once I arrived at the emergency room, the attending doctor leaned over, looked at me, and said, "You have had a stroke on the right side of your brain, and it has affected the left side of your body. You will be paralyzed for the rest of your life."

I looked at him and shook my head no. He looked at me and stated, "This happens to many stroke patients. They first deny and refuse to admit what is happening."

I had peace and a praise that God was with me and that He was in control of the situation.

The doctor ordered a series of tests EKG, MRI, and blood test. My nephew called my husband in New York City to tell him about my condition. I could hear my husband on speakerphone saying he was taking the next plane, but I muttered, "No, God said He was going to heal me; you will waste a plane ticket!"

During this time, I noticed that I had no control over my swallowing mechanism and forming words. I knew what I wanted to say but needed help expressing it. My husband and family mentioned to me after the ordeal that they couldn't understand what I was saying on the phone. However, they didn't want to tell me. My daughter-in-law told me that she remembered me saying, "Hallelujah."

I began to cry with praise and joy. My doctor came into my room and asked how my vision was and cautioned me that I couldn't eat because my swallowing mechanism was not working properly and that I may need a feeding tube if there was no improvement. She also mentioned that it was too late for the speech therapist to come; he was gone for the day, and the test had to be done in the morning. I muttered to my nephew, "I WILL NOT HAVE A FEEDING TUBE!" Immediately, my mind went back to when my mother had a massive heart attack and stroke many years ago and had to be placed on a feeding tube. I said to myself, "I'm not going out like that. I will live and not die."

As I began to fall asleep, I was woken up by the nurse and was given a breathing tube; she expressed it was for precaution and a breathing device that I had to blow into to measure my breathing pressure. I fell into a deep sleep, but at 2:00 am, I was woken up by a shake on my left arm, the same way as the morning of the stroke. I looked around and thought it was my nephew, but he was asleep. As I tried to gain my vision because of the room's darkness, I heard the voice of the Lord tell me, "Take off the sackcloth because what I'm getting ready to do in your body doesn't represent what you have on." I had a hospital gown on, and there was a beautiful sundress that my niece had given me the day before. The Lord said, "Put it on." I knew immediately that I had to get up and obey God, but I looked at my body and the wristband on my arm, which was written "FALL RISK," and proceeded to scoot back and forth, trying to get out of the bed.

Because of my sudden movements, I woke up my nephew, and he said, "What are you doing, Auntie? You can't get out of bed. You are going to fall!"

It was then that I knew something supernatural was about to happen. I began pointing to the sundress, and he looked at me and said, "You want to get dressed? It's two in the morning; Uncle Glenn will kill me if you fall!"

By this time, the nurse on the night shift walked in and expressed great concern that she could lose her job if she allowed me to get up without the doctor's permission. They helped me into the bathroom, and as she began to bathe me in the tub, I began to speak the word of God out of my mouth. Psalm 91, 27, and 23, and I continued to speak the word of God as the water poured over my body I shall live and not die, I shall live and not die, I shall live and not die and declare the works of the Lord Psalms 118:17! As the nurse dressed me, I could feel the muscles in my extremities begin to feel like balloons. It felt like the word of God became the breath of healing in my body.

Then I heard the voice of the Lord say, "Go to the mirror and put on your make-up." It was when I realized God became my physical therapist.

Unfortunately, as I attempted to put lipstick on, my right arm was too weak to stand in position, and this is when I saw my face for the first time. My lips and face were twisted, and I had difficulty swallowing my salvia.

The nurse was standing behind me, jumping back and saying, "OMG, your face looks normal now!"

I saw the transformation myself. Then God spoke to me and said, "Walk around the hospital ward six times."

I looked at my nephew and pointed to the door. The nurse had left the room, and my nephew had disconnected me from the oxygen tube earlier. I proceeded out of my hospital room, down the wall with an IV in my arm and the IV bag on a pole with wheels. At this time, my nephew seemed a little nervous and called my husband, and he told him everything that had taken place.

I heard my husband tell him, "Listen....my wife is a woman of God; whatever she tells you to do, do it."

Walking around the hospital ward, I noticed other stroke patients curled up in their beds like caterpillars, but I was pushing and speaking God's word. I had walked around the ward a couple of times, struggling but pushing to speak God's word, "I shall live and not die."

But I kept walking. At one point in the middle of my walk, my nephew stated, "Auntie, you sound better, and your words are clearer!"

This was the first time anyone told me that my words were slurred. By this time, I could feel the strength come back into my body. During the last round of my walk, I was walking and talking. The nurse was amazed at what had happened. I returned to my hospital bed to rest until morning, praising God for what had just happened. At 9:00 am, the physical therapist was amazed, watching me walk around the room and do jumping jacks. Then around 10:00 am, the speech therapist came; she told me she had another patient but was told by the physical therapist that she must see a patient in Room 702. She told me in tears that her father had the same stroke I had two months ago and did not survive.

She looked me in my eyes and said, "I don't think you realized that you just had a stroke that people do not recover from. Mrs. McBride, you are a miracle. I just buried my father."

The speech therapist told me she had to do a series of tests to see if I needed a feeding tube. I told her that if God could restore my left-side paralysis, I would not have a feeding tube. She looked at me and stated, "Because you can move doesn't mean you can swallow." She explained that she would give me four different types of food: one spoon of apple sauce, one spoon of Jello, and one spoon of pudding. Then, I half a cookie with water after each swallow, and if I swallowed each one with success, I could eat. As she was getting the items together, I began to pray and hold on to faith.

By only God's grace and mercy, I could swallow each item. My doctor was called, and she asked me who woke me up yesterday morning when I had the stroke. I told her no one was around when I felt the shake on my left shoulder. She told me that if I didn't wake up and remained asleep, I would have been left out. She told me, "Mrs. McBride, God woke you up." She gave me a complete examination and a clean build of health. Before I was released, she told me that she and a team of doctors had come to my room the night before. She was looking at me because she was puzzled. After all, I exercised, ate healthily, and all blood tests were regular. But she mentioned that God reminded her of an article she read two months ago in a medical journal about an enzyme in the liver that produces much cholesterol in the liver. The enzyme is hereditary, from both mother and father, and a special test must be administered; a regular cholesterol test will not detect this enzyme. My doctor requested that I have the blood test, which showed I tested positive for the enzyme. She explained that exercise and eating healthy do not eliminate this enzyme. It's only controlled by a medication called a statin.

God had me in the right state, in the right hospital, with the right doctor. Through God's grace and mercy, I was able to fly back to New York City, restored by God's supernatural intervention, living a full productive life with family and ministry. I will live and not die.

Acknowledgments

This endeavor would not have been possible without the prayers and support of my husband, Dr. Glenn A. McBride Sr., family, and friends. I extend gratitude and appreciation to Dr. Pastor Elaine Harvey, the visionary, Apostle Deborah Allen, the publisher, the amazing literary team, and co-authors. I am deeply indebted to everyone who purchases this book, knowing that the written word will change and transform their lives.

DR. JUIET PINDER-MCBRIDE

About Dr. Juliet Pinder-McBride

Dr. McBride is the Co-Founder of McBride Ministries. Dr. McBride is the teacher of Sister God-given ministry that mentors and teaches women their God given purpose. GIRL TALK is a program by New York City Police Department which has given Sister Talk the opportunity to teach young girls life skills, positive self-esteem, healthy living, and wellness. She graduated from Norman Thomas High School NYC.

Dr. McBride also graduated from Lehman College with her BA in Psychology. She is a member of the National Honor Society of Psi Chi in Psychology and a member of the National Society of Morani Shujaa in African Studies. Dr. McBride continued her education and graduated from Boricua College Master's in English as a New Language. She was ordained Pastor in 2007 by Bishop I.V. Hilliard New Light Christian Church in Houston, TX. In addition, Dr. McBride received her Doctor of Divinity from Saint Thomas Christian University in 2017.

Dr. McBride has been an educator, intervention reading specialist, and related service provider for 23 years for the New York City Department of Education. She is a board member of "Bright Future Children After School Center."

She is also a board member of the Bahamian Association of NYC; the paternal grandmother Alice Pinder was the only female founder on the board of eight men; she was an immigrant from Eleuthera, Bahamas.

Dr. McBride belongs to various groups and organizations such as the Women on a Mission NYC,

DR. JUIET PINDER-MCBRIDE

Purpose Driven Ladiez outreach and mentoring program, Pastor's W.I.V.E.S Ministries, Board member of Ruth Sisters Fellowship International as Membership Director and a Member of the 1000 Women in Religion and Global Peace at the United Nations NYC.

Dr. McBride and her husband have partnered with many ministries, building schools and feeding homeless children and orphans in the Dominican Republic and Haiti named Trabjando Para Cristo Levantando al Caido (Working for Christ Lifting the Fallen.)

Dr. McBride has partnered with The National Coalitional of 100 Black Women LI, Hope & Heroes Children's Cancer Fund at Columbia University, Educational Director and Supervisor of Bronx Works After school for Arts, Literacy and STEM, Alliance for Lupus Research, Witness Walk Cancer Awareness, ABBA Leadership Center.

She is an author of Amazon's 7x Bestseller and 3xs New Release of a book entitled, "RISE UP" "Women Who Lead Building Legacy."

Dr. McBride and her husband, Dr. Glenn A. McBride Sr., have been married for 41 years and are the proud parents of three sons, Glenn Jr., 39, Jonathan, 35, and Jason, 30, one daughter-in-love, and four grandchildren.

Contact information:

I AM AN OVERCOMER, I SURVIVED!

Facebook: Juliet Pinder-McBride
Email Address: ladymcbride2@hotmail.com

Made in the USA
Middletown, DE
10 May 2023